W9-BPJ-103

© Copyright Academy of Surfing Instructors Pty Ltd 2004

Published by the Academy of Surfing Instructors Pty Ltd
406/136 Curlewis Street,
Bondi, New South Wales, 2026 Australia

First published: October 2004

National Library of Australia
Cataloguing-in-Publication data:

ISBN 0-9751523-1-9
Learn to Surf – Intermediate level

Surfing is a dangerous sport. All care has been taken to give the best possible
advice in this instruction manual. No responsibility is accepted for any illnesses
or injuries incurred by an individual when following the directions contained in
this instruction manual. Any injuries resulting from surfing are the sole
responsibility of the individual who wilfully and knowingly engages in a sport
known to be dangerous.

Forward

by Nigel Hutton-Potts

I started surfing at the age of 6 on an inflated rubber surf mat. The only trouble was, when I stood up, the mat would bend in the middle so there was little chance of keeping up with the curl. I did all that I could to catch, and stay with, those waves.

From there I progressed to a coolite foam board. I seemed to be able to have a bit more direction. Even though I didn't have a fin, I could use the rails of the board to cut along the wave and stay with the curl.

After about three years on the coolite foamie, I got a fibre-glass surfboard. I was stoked. It was big to me (but only 5ft 10"). It was a Gordon and Woods diamond tail single fin. The board was smoother, faster. I had positive direction (due to the fin) and now I could make sections on the wave that I could never get to before and perform real manoeuvres.

I was hooked on surfing. I loved riding the waves. I didn't have to have the best wave. It was enough just to catch any wave.

For those of you who have the same feeling and have become hooked, I hope this instruction manual can help you gain solid skills at the intermediate level. All too often, learning to surf can sometimes be "trial and error" and/or "information overload". This manual has been written to allow you to develop your skills naturally before moving onto the advanced level.

Be kind to the ocean for it is the surfer's playground and home to many beautiful creatures.

Nigel has been surfing for over 30 years and is experienced in all aspects of surfing. He grew up in Bondi Beach, Australia and has devoted his life to surfing surf breaks around the world.

Nigel provides the "inside" on what surfing is all about and a wealth of tips and techniques, gained over the years, on the "how" to surf at all levels.

About this Instruction Manual

This manual is the second in a series of Learn to Surf manuals produced by the Academy of Surfing Instructors. It aims to assist people to gain the necessary skills and knowledge required to surf with competence at the intermediate level.

The information provided in this manual builds on the information provided in the *Learn to Surf for Beginners* manual. It is assumed the learner has read the *Learn to Surf for Beginners* manual and has the skills and knowledge at the beginner's level.

Contributors

We would like to thank the following for their contribution to this manual:

Ripcurl www.ripcurl.com
FCS www.fincontrol.com
Gorilla Grip www.g-grip.com
Speeedfins www.speeedfins.com
Rodney Dahlberg Surfboards
Channel Island Surfboards www.cisurfboards.com

CONTENTS

Academy of Surfing Instructors (ASI)

The Academy of Surfing Instructors (ASI) is a surfing education organisation. ASI provides a full range of educational materials to assist surfers to gain surfing skills and knowledge from beginner to Instructor level.

All ASI training programs meet sound educational standards. Certificates of Achievement can be issued should the participant wish to be assessed as competent at the designated surf skill level.

Contact us on +61 2 9365 4170
(In Australia - Ph: 02 9365 4170)
email: info@academyofsurfing.com

See our website:
www.academyofsurfing.com

Setting the world standard in surfing education

Introduction

Congratulations on embarking on the *Learn to Surf - Intermediate Level*. At the beginners level you would have had some fun, learned to stand to your feet and wobbled back to the shore whilst trying to maintain dignity and balance!

Now you're over that and onto the next level. A far more exciting and enjoyable stage of your new life as a surfer. This is where you are ready to move along the face of the wave and learn how to put in practice some of your basic foundation principles and get into doing a few new, fun manoeuvres.

In this manual, we will cover topics such as assessing weather and surf conditions, your surfboard and surf clothing – what works and what doesn't. Also covered are techniques that help you to find the surf, so you can catch that ultimate ride. We go into more depth on surf skill techniques to allow you to further perfect your skills and then provide you with step-by-step descriptions on how to perform some hot manoeuvres.

So let's wax up and catch some waves.....

Chapter 1
Assessing Surfing Conditions

Outcomes

1. Access and interpret meteorological information and determine surfing activity once you have considered weather information.

Will the surf be pumping today and where will it be best?

These two questions constantly occupy the surfer's mind in the never ending pursuit of the perfect ride. Developing the skills to assess where the surf will be and the likely surf conditions are, therefore, necessary skills to develop so you don't miss out!

There are a number of factors that contribute to you being able to assess where the surf is and the likely surf conditions.

These are:
- the weather
- swell
- tides
- wind direction and speed
- water and wave conditions

Local knowledge is also required so that you can apply the above factors to the local surf break.

Let's have a look at these factors in more depth.

1. The Weather

The weather plays the most important part in deciding surf conditions. Being able to understand weather information and interpret weather maps all help in your success to find where the surf will be best.

Weather information can also be obtained from a number of places including television, radio, newspapers and internet sites. Weather information comes in different shapes and forms.

You are probably familiar with the weather reports presented with the news on the television. These reports usually provide weather maps with the land and sea temperature, rain conditions and show high and low pressure systems. The amount of information provided can vary. These weather reports provide a useful guide to weather conditions. However, just keep in mind, that there are many other factors that also contribute to forecasting weather conditions accurately.

Reading weather maps is a skill that can be acquired by anyone. It is a good idea for every aspiring surfer to gain this skill. Check out the weather reports and see what the affect is on your local surf. You will soon start to predict the surf conditions with relative accuracy.

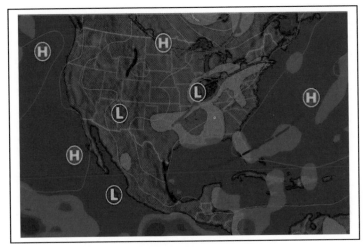

Weather Map - USA
(Reference: CNN.com www.CNN/WEATHER.com)

When reading weather maps, take note of the high and low pressure systems. Low pressure systems are identified by the letter "L" and produce the strongest winds. As mentioned in the *Learn to Surf for Beginners* instruction manual, wind is the main factor for creating waves. Low pressure systems are usually associated with cooler weather, storms and even cyclones / tornados / typhoons.

High pressure systems are identified by the letter "H" and produce little or no wind. These systems are usually associated with warm to hot weather with sunny summer conditions.

To find out if there are going to be waves, check for low pressure systems on the weather forecasts and maps.

Also have a look to see how many isobars are present. (Isobars are the lines drawn around high and low pressure systems). The closer the isobars, the stronger the wind will be. This also means there is more likelihood of large waves.

The wind direction is also determined by high and low pressures. In the southern hemisphere, air flows clockwise around low pressure systems and anti-clockwise around high pressure systems. The opposite applies to the northern hemisphere.

High and low pressure systems move from west to east or other directions depending on where you are in the world. This allows you to predict what the weather could be like a few days in the future.

Surf Study - Reading
Weather Maps

Have a look at the weather map, of Australia, below. There are both high and low pressure systems on this map. The low pressure systems are on the west and east coast. As a result, there may be swell on both of these coasts.

The swell on the west coast will probably be smaller than on the east coast. The low pressure system on the east coast has isobars closer together which means stronger winds and therefore potentially larger swell.

The high pressure system in the west (on the edge of the map) will move across Australia to the east and also push the low further east, away from the land. As a result of this, there may be little surf, in two to three days times, unless another low pressure system comes in and pushes the high away.

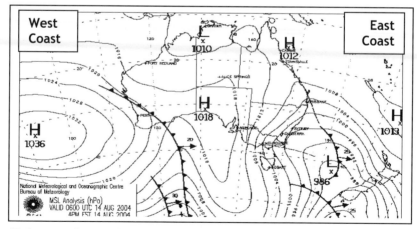

(Reference: Bureau of Meteorology Australia. www.bom.gov.au)

2. Swell

Swell is the formation of waves. Without swell, there will be no waves.

There are two types of swell:
1. ground swell
2. wind swell

2.1 Ground Swell

Ground swell is generated by wind from strong deep low pressure systems out at sea. The swell can travel long distances (kilometres/miles) before it reaches the shore and can continue for days.

Ground swell is recognisable by distinct, clear lines of swell. There may or may not be wind with a ground swell.

Ground swell is the better type of swell to surf. It often produces cleaner, larger and more consistent waves.

A ground swell.
Notice the lines.

2.2 Wind Swell

Wind swell is generated by the wind from local storms.

You could have wind for about 4 hours. This can whip up a 3 metre (6 foot) swell and then as the wind dies down or changes, the swell will disappear.

You can identify wind swell as it is always accompanied by wind. The swell is also moving in the same direction as the wind (usually an on-shore wind).

Wind swell is generally choppy with uneven lines - i.e. the lines of swell are not straight but come into the shore with varying angles, with waves peaking in different places.

If the wind continues for a long enough time, and blows strong enough, it will eventually form into a ground swell.

3. Tides

Tides are another factor in determining surf conditions. Tides result due to the gravitational pull of the moon. The ocean rises and falls approximately every 6 ½ to 7 hours and as a result has a major affect on wave conditions.

In 24 hours, there are approximately 2 high tides and 2 low tides. As tides change approximately every 6 ½ to 7 hours, the high and low tide will be slightly different on each day. For example, the high tide may be at 9 am today and then tomorrow, it will be at approximately 10 am.

At low tide, there is less water over a break and at high tide there is more water. The depth of the water affects wave formation. As discussed in the *Learn to Surf for Beginners* manual, as the swell enters shallow water, the compression of the swell forces the water to rise up until it reaches a point where the top throws over as a breaking wave.

| At high tide, this surf break is the perfect place to surf with good waves. | At low tide, this same surf break reveals a rocky bottom with the waves barely breaking. |

If a particular wave is closing out at low tide, it is more likely to be breaking, with a better shape, at high tide. This is because there is more water over the shore at high tide. If you check the surf and see that the waves are closing out, and you notice that it is close to low tide, you will know that it will break better later, or that it was breaking better earlier. At the higher tide, there will be more water over the surf break. Therefore, it is less likely to close-out.

The moon also has another affect on tides. Generally, when there is a full moon, or new moon, there tends to be more swell and slightly higher tides.

On an incoming tide, the waves are also assisted by the pushing effect of the tide and the waves get slightly higher and sometimes more consistent than on a dropping tide (a tide that is running out).

Usually, you will notice that it is better to surf on a mid to medium tide that is rising towards the high tide and/or for a few hours after the high tide.

Deciding whether to surf on an incoming, higher, or an outgoing, lower tide depends on a number of factors including the size of the swell and the depth of water over the break.

3.1 Tide Charts

Tide charts are very useful in showing you when the tides are high and low and when the full moon will occur. This will assist in planning when to go surfing. If you are a planning a surfing trip to another location, you can plan the days when the tides will be the most favourable for producing the best waves, given the conditions. You will also need to have an understanding of what tide works best at that particular location.

Tide charts show the size of the tide for each hour of daylight on a given day, in a given month. The size of the tide will be measured in either metres or feet, depending on the country. Each page usually shows one month and then each day is listed. The time is listed across the top of the page. The times are generally numbered according to the 24 hour clock. e.g. 17 would be 5.00 pm. Tide charts are usually printed over a 12 month period.

Tides are different in different parts of the world. The tide chart will show the tides at a particular location.

You can usually obtain tide charts free of charge from surf shops/schools and fishing shops. You can also check out the local newspaper or weather reports.

DATE	5	6	7	8	9	10	11	12	13	14	15	16	17	18	19
Tue 1	1.2	1.6	2.0	2.3	2.4	2.2	1.9	1.5	1.0	0.6	0.4	0.4	0.6	0.9	1.3
Wed 2	1.0	1.4	1.8	2.2	2.5	2.5	2.2	1.8	1.3	0.8	0.4	0.2	0.3	0.6	1.0
Thu 3	0.8	1.1	1.6	2.1	2.4	2.6	2.5	2.1	1.6	1.0	0.5	0.2	0.1	0.3	0.6
Fri 4	0.6	0.9	1.3	1.8	2.3	2.6	2.6	2.4	1.9	1.4	0.8	0.3	0.1	0.1	0.4
Sat 5	0.6	0.7	1.1	1.6	2.0	2.4	2.6	2.5	2.2	1.7	1.1	0.6	0.2	0.1	0.2
Sun 6	0.7	0.7	0.9	1.3	1.7	2.2	2.5	2.6	2.4	2.0	1.5	0.9	0.4	0.2	0.1
Mon 7	0.9	0.7	0.8	1.0	1.4	1.9	2.2	2.4	2.4	2.2	1.8	1.2	0.7	0.4	0.2
Tue 8	1.1	0.9	0.8	0.9	1.2	1.5	1.9	2.2	2.3	2.2	2.0	1.5	1.1	0.7	0.4
Wed 9	1.3	1.1	0.9	0.9	1.0	1.3	1.6	1.9	2.1	2.1	2.0	1.7	1.4	1.0	0.7
Thu 10	1.6	1.4	1.2	1.0	1.0	1.1	1.3	1.5	1.7	1.9	1.9	1.8	1.6	1.3	1.0
Fri 11	1.8	1.6	1.4	1.2	1.1	1.0	1.1	1.2	1.4	1.6	1.7	1.7	1.7	1.5	1.3
Sat 12	1.9	1.8	1.7	1.5	1.3	1.1	1.0	1.0	1.1	1.2	1.4	1.5	1.6	1.6	1.5
Sun 13	1.8	2.0	2.0	1.8	1.6	1.3	1.1	0.9	0.9	0.9	1.0	1.2	1.4	1.5	1.6
Mon 14	1.7	2.0	2.1	2.1	1.9	1.6	1.3	1.0	0.8	0.7	0.7	0.9	1.1	1.4	1.5
Tue 15	1.5	1.9	2.1	2.3	2.2	2.0	1.6	1.2	0.8	0.6	0.5	0.6	0.8	1.1	1.4
Wed 16	1.3	1.7	2.0	2.3	2.4	2.2	1.9	1.5	1.0	0.6	0.4	0.3	0.5	0.8	1.1
Thu 17	1.0	1.4	1.9	2.2	2.5	2.5	2.2	1.8	1.3	0.8	0.4	0.2	0.2	0.5	0.8
Fri 18	0.8	1.2	1.6	2.0	2.4	2.5	2.5	2.2	1.7	1.1	0.6	0.2	0.1	0.2	0.5
Sat 19	0.7	0.9	1.3	1.8	2.2	2.5	2.6	2.4	2.0	1.5	0.9	0.4	0.1	0.1	0.3
Sun 20	0.7	0.8	1.0	1.5	1.9	2.3	2.5	2.5	2.3	1.8	1.2	0.7	0.3	0.1	0.1
Mon 21	0.8	0.7	0.9	1.2	1.6	2.0	2.4	2.5	2.4	2.1	1.6	1.0	0.5	0.2	0.1
Tue 22	1.0	0.8	0.8	1.0	1.3	1.7	2.1	2.3	2.4	2.2	1.8	1.3	0.8	0.4	0.2
Wed 23	1.2	1.0	0.8	0.8	1.0	1.4	1.7	2.0	2.2	2.2	2.0	1.6	1.2	0.7	0.4
Thu 24	1.5	1.2	1.0	0.9	0.9	1.1	1.4	1.7	1.9	2.1	2.0	1.8	1.4	1.0	0.7
Fri 25	1.7	1.5	1.2	1.0	0.9	1.0	1.1	1.4	1.6	1.8	1.9	1.8	1.6	1.3	1.0
Sat 26	1.9	1.8	1.5	1.3	1.1	1.0	1.0	1.1	1.3	1.5	1.6	1.7	1.6	1.5	1.3
Sun 27	2.0	2.0	1.8	1.6	1.3	1.1	0.8	0.9	1.3	1.1	1.3	1.5	1.5	1.5	1.4
Mon 28	1.9	2.1	2.0	1.9	1.6	1.3	1.1	0.9	0.8	0.8	1.0	1.1	1.3	1.5	1.5
Tue 29	1.8	2.0	2.2	2.1	1.9	1.7	1.3	1.0	0.7	0.6	0.7	0.8	1.0	1.3	1.4
Wed 30	1.6	1.9	2.2	2.3	2.2	2.0	1.6	1.2	0.9	0.6	0.5	0.5	0.7	1.0	1.3

● new moon   ● full moon

Billabong. TIDE CHART

3.1.1 How to Read a Tide Chart

Go to the relevant month on the tide chart. The month will usually be printed on each page. Next, find the relevant day and date. These are usually displayed down the left hand side of the page.

For example, let's go to the first entry in the tide chart shown on the previous page 8 – Tuesday 1st June. This information is reproduced below, from the tide chart:

TIME AM	5	6	7	8	9	10	11	12
Tues 1	1.2	1.6	2.0	2.3	2.4	2.2	1.9	1.5

TIME PM	13	14	15	16	17	18	19
Tues 1	1.0	0.6	0.4	0.4	0.6	0.9	1.3

These figures measure the size of tide. The lowest figure along this line will correspond to low tide and the highest figure along that line will be the high tide of the day.

In our example: we can see that high tide is at 9 hundred hours (9 am in the morning) and low tide is at 15/16 hundred hours (3pm / 4 pm in the afternoon).

We could guess that high tide would occur again at approximately 21 hundred hours (9 pm at night) – 6 ½ hours later and low tide at approximately 3 hundred hours (3 am in the morning).

The first "time" entry (at 5 am) shows a lower tide of 1.2. We have estimated that low tide would have been at approximately 3 am so at 5 am the tide is just past low tide. You can see the figures progressively increasing until high tide is reached at 9 am. The figures then progressively decrease until 15 hundred hours (3 pm - the lowest tide) and then progressively start to increase again.

Around the full and new moon, the figures will tend to increase to a high tide that will be larger than the tides during the middle of the moon phase. The new/full moon tides usually mean the swell size will increase as the gravitational pull of the moon is stronger during these peak moon phases.

In the tide chart shown above, the full moon is on Wed 2nd. The tide is highest at 9/10 hundred hours (9 am in the morning) with a tide measuring 2.5. The new moon is on Thu 17th with a high tide at 9/10 hundred hours (9am / 10 am in the morning) also measuring 2.5. These tides are the highest points in the whole month.

In between the full and new moon, the highest tide is much lower. For example, on Thurs 10th, the highest tide is only 1.9.

Tide charts may also be displayed in an abbreviated format. In this example, not all the hours of the daylight days are shown. Only the 2 low tides and 2 high tides are shown. In addition, the 24 hour clock is not used.

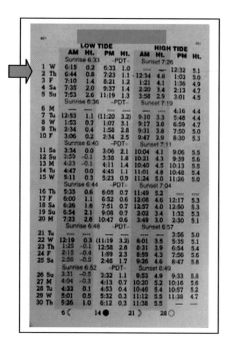

If we look at the entry – 2 Th, we can see:

- Low tide occurs at 6.44 am and 7.23 pm
- High tide occurs at 12.34 am and 1.03 pm

3.2 Tide Watch

Some surfers also wear watches that have a tide dial. The tide dial shows high/low tide and whether the tide is rising or falling. You simply set the watch according to the tide chart and then you will be able work out what the tide is doing when checking the surf or even when you are out in the surf.

4. Wind Direction and Speed

When we talk about wind direction in surfing terms, we are talking about where the wind is blowing in relation to the land mass. The wind direction always has an impact on surf conditions.

4.1 Wind Direction

The three main types of wind direction are:
- On-shore wind
- Off-shore wind
- Cross-shore wind

4.1.1 On-shore Wind

Wind that blows from the ocean to the land (i.e. to the shore / coast / beach). Generally on-shore wind flattens the wave, causing the top of the waves to lose their shape, crumble and not hold up cleanly.

4.1.2 Off-shore Wind

Wind that blows from the land to the ocean. If the wind is strong, you can see the spray blowing off the wave lip and out to sea. The off-shore wind helps the wave face to stand up before peeling over cleanly. It can often create a hollow in the wave. Hollow waves are ideal for tube rides.

4.1.3 Cross-shore Wind

Wind that blows sideways across the incoming surf. A cross-shore wind can be good if you are surfing a right hand-break and the wind is cross-shore from left to right (when looking at the surf from the beach). However, it could cause the left to close out or crumble (as in the photo shown). The opposite applies if the wind is blowing from the other direction.

4.2 Wind Speed

The speed of the wind also affects the condition of the surf. If wind speed is too high, it will blow the surf out and make it a large, unrideable mess.

On most mornings, when there are no strong weather conditions prevailing, there will be a slight off-shore wind or no wind at all.

Wind tends to go from the land, which has cooled off over night, and out to sea, which has been warmed by the sun in the early morning. (Remember your science studies – cool air moves to take the place of warm air). Then, by around 10 am in the morning, the land will start to warm up more than the sea. The wind will change direction to go from the cooler sea and onto the land, creating an on-shore wind.

Late afternoon/early evening is also the time that wind will blow off-shore or become calm. This is also a good time to surf.

As mentioned previously, weather maps and reports can give you an indication of wind speed and direction.

CHAPTER 2
Where to Find the Surf

Outcomes

☐   Identify different types of surf breaks.

1. Surf Breaks

In the last chapter, we looked at how the weather, swell, wind and tides affect surf conditions. Once you have looked at whether there will be any swell, you can head to your surf break (or check internet surf cams) to see if the waves are breaking. There are five main types of places where the surf breaks. These are:
* beach break
* point break
* reef break
* bombora
* river mouth

1.1 Beach Break

Beach breaks are the most common break. You will find beach breaks on exposed beaches where swell is coming in. The break occurs due to sandbanks under the surface of the water.

Beach breaks are the easiest to access and are generally safer in terms of wiping out. However, sandbanks shift around with wind and water currents resulting in the waves changing from one surf to the next. The surf may be great one day and breaking nicely. Then the next day, the surf could be closing out. The quality of the wave is determined by the shape of the sandbank.

If the waves are dumping and closing out, it generally means the sandbank is built up in a straight line along the coast with no distinct channels. This is not suitable for surfing. Try to find a beach with triangular sandbanks. This means the waves will peel in forming left and right hand waves (more suitable for surfing).

1.2 Point Break

A point break is where the surf breaks off a headland. A point break also breaks over reef and/or rock formations.

Point breaks generally provide waves of more uniform shape allowing you to be better able to predict where the wave will break. Due to the consistency of the waves, point breaks are a more desirable type of break for surfing.

This type of break can be dangerous as there can be many submerged rocks. If you get wiped out, you run the risk of hitting the rocks. Make sure you dive shallow at these breaks and be aware of the location of potentially dangerous rocks.

1.3 Reef Break

A reef break is where waves break over a submerged reef or rock formation. Like a point break, the waves have consistent form when they break.

Reef breaks are dangerous as the water can be quite shallow. This is more so at low tide when the reef or rock formation is close to the surface of the water. Rock reef is generally smoother. Coral reef is generally sharper and therefore even more dangerous for wipe-outs.

1.4 Bombora

The bombora ("bombie") is submerged rock or reef formation that occurs off the edge of the coastline. As the swell hits the shallow water, waves are formed. Bombora's can occur many kilometres (miles) from the shore.

Bombora's are generally known for their big waves that will usually be surfed by "tow-in". That is, the surfers are towed into the wave by a jet ski.

The waves may also be smaller on the bombora so that a jet ski is not necessary.

1.5 River Mouth

The river mouth break occurs where the river meets the sea. The waves are often good as the constant flow of water out of the river, into the sea, creates a channel with banks built up of rock and sand that has been washed out from the river over many years.

When it rains heavily, after a period of no rain, it is a good idea to give the river mouth break a miss for at least a day, until the river flushes out any pollutants and debris.

Chapter 3
How to "Read" Waves

Outcomes

☐ Identify water conditions suitable for surfing.
☐ Identify different wave types and their suitability for surfing.
☐ Determine whether a wave is left or right.
☐ Describe wave frequency.

The waves are your playing field. Each wave is different. Understanding the different water and wave conditions is a skill that is essential to perfecting your surfing skills.

You cannot always predict what a wave will do but if you have a good understanding of different wave types, it will assist you to choose and ride waves that are suitable to your surfing skill. Over time, you will be able to identify different types of wave conditions and their suitability for surfing.

Let's have a look at the different types of water and wave conditions.

1. Water Conditions

Before getting out into the surf, check out the water conditions. The weather, wind and tides combined create water conditions that make it ideal for surfing or, on the other hand, can make it downright unpleasant.

1.1 Glassy

The term "glassy" describes the most ideal water conditions to surf in. The water is very smooth as there is very little or no wind. The water appears glassy as the light glistens and reflects off the water surface. This condition allows your surfboard to easily glide over the waves.

1.2 Wind Blown

Also known as mushie, messy, choppy, out of control. These waves are the opposite of glassy water conditions. There is generally lots of wind blowing either across or on-shore, resulting in the wave losing its form. The waves do not have a smooth face to do manoeuvres. They are generally not good for surfing.

1.3 Lumpy

Lumpy water is where there are bumps and ripples in the wave. It occurs where there is lots of backwash, chop or wind. Lumpy waves are more difficult to ride. In this photo, a cross-shore wind is blowing causing the crest and face of the wave to be uneven.

1.4 Backwash

Backwash happens when a wave reaches the shore, washes up the beach or into the land and then forms back into a wave again as it washes back out to sea. Beware of places where backwash is occurring as they make waves jump straight up as the incoming and outgoing wave hit each other. If you are riding a wave and see a backwash wave coming towards you, be prepared for a sudden lift up in the wave.

You can easily see backwash in surf. As a backwash hits an incoming wave it will rise up for a second, sometimes throwing water high into the air.

1.5 Water Hazards

Check the water for any potential hazards. We covered many of these in the *Learn to Surf for Beginners* manual.

Hazards include pollution, tree branches, coconuts, seaweed and any other debris that may be floating in the water. City beaches sometimes have a lot of street litter washed into the water especially if there has been heavy rain. You may think twice about going out into this type of water.

Otter in water

Depending on where you surf, there may also be sea animals such as seals, otters, turtles and dolphins. Generally, these sea creatures will keep out of your way. Some other sea creatures may not be so harmless. Before going surfing, check the beach to see if there are any blue bottles or stingers lying on the shore. Often on-shore winds blow these closer to shore.

Most often, the major hazard when surfing is other people. Check for swimmers, beginner surfers and surf craft such as boogie boards, surf ski's and kayaks, to make sure you can surf safely amongst them.

Avoid any man-made surf hazards such as piers.

2. Types of Waves

2.1 The Best Wave for Surfing

Let's have a look at what makes a wave suitable for riding. How do you judge if one wave is better to ride than another wave?

As a beginner, you were looking for waves that were gently breaking. You probably even surfed the whitewash in an effort to perfect your beginner's surfing skills.

At the intermediate level, you will be looking at the wave form. The way a wave "forms up". This will determine how long your ride will be and what manoeuvres you will be able to perform.

A well formed wave is a wave that is "walling up". In other words, the face of the wave will stand up (form) cleanly, and be gently peeling over from left to right or right to left. In this instance, the wave is said to be "peeling off" (breaking perfectly).

✔ **Good wave form**
The wave is peeling over
and walling up in front
of the surfer.

A good wave will also have some amount of fall (drop) to it. The drop allows you to surf down the wave and gather speed to go back up the wave. We will talk more about how you do this in the Manoeuvres chapter of this manual. If the wave is walling up, it will have a natural drop.

Below are some examples of bad wave form:

✗ **Bad wave form**

Is a close out (dumper). This is where the wave face breaks all at once. There is nowhere to ride along the face of the wave.

✗ **Bad wave form**

These waves are small, erratic and uneven.

✗ **Bad wave form**

This wave is closing out in front of the surfer. The surfer will have no wall to surf on – only whitewash.

✗ **Bad wave form**
Wave face has faded (diminished). These waves are not good to surf as the waves do not have the energy to push you along and no drop to generate speed. As such you will lose momentum and come to a stop in the water.

Waves generally tend to fade when they move into deeper water. As discussed in the *Learn to Surf for Beginners* manual, one of the factors that cause waves to rise up is the compression of water particles as they enter into shallower water. As the wave then moves into deeper water, the water particles are not as compressed and hence the wave loses its form.

Waves can fade and then wall up again. As the wave travels into the shore, it can move over deeper channels (fade out) and then over shallower sandbanks or reef (build up again).

Being able to identify where the channels and sandbanks are will also give you an indication of how the waves will form as they travel into the shore.

Look out for rips and currents. Good waves tend to break beside rips or currents. This is because the wave can break along the edge of the deeper water (the channel).

The suitability of the waves will also depend on your level of skill and your ability to read the wave as you are riding it.

For example, you may notice that a wave walls up nicely in front of you. Then it hits a channel and starts to fade. It will then start to wall up again as it moves over a sandbank. You may determine that if you surf to a particular place on the wave, you may be able to ride through the fading section and onto the wall again. In a matter of seconds, you will assess whether you have the skill to make the manoeuvre and whether the wave can support that manoeuvre. The more you surf, the better your judgement will become.

2.2 Other Wave Types

Below are some other types of waves that occur that may or may not make the wave suitable for surfing.

2.2.1 Sucky

Sucky waves generally occur alongside channels, where a fast moving rip is rushing out to sea. The water rushing out to sea hits the incoming wave and has nowhere to go but up, and over, the wave. The movement of the outgoing water causes the water to be "sucked" out and up and over the wave. This creates a much faster continuous drop down the wave face.

You can see if the waves are sucky by checking for any rip or current moving out to sea. Check if other surfers out the back are paddling into the shore to stay in position. This also indicates that the waves will be sucky.

When you are riding the wave, the effect of a strong rip or current can be felt in waves. If you are surfing on the wave, you feel that you are going much faster than you would normally be.

The faster the rip/current, the more sucky the waves will be. i.e. more water rushing up over the wave face.

These waves are ideal for surfing as the continuous wall (drop) allows you to perform manoeuvres. However, the waves could be sucky and still not have good shape. Check for rips/currents and how fast they are moving and whether the wave has good form.

Sucky waves are generally found on beach breaks. Also, cross currents/rips can cause waves to be sucky at other breaks.

2.2.2 Hollow

Hollow refers to a wave that stands up before throwing over (breaking). A space is created between the wave face and the water that is throwing over. Hollow breaking waves are usually assisted by an off-shore wind. The wind blowing off the shore hits the incoming wave causing the wave to be "hollow". Hollow waves are ideal for getting tube rides.

2.2.3 Spitting

Spitting occurs when a wave is tubing. As the wave shuts down, the air and water vapour trapped inside the tube is compressed, throwing air and water out the end of the tube as a fine spray. The spray is referred to as "spitting".

If you see waves that are spitting, this indicates that the wave is ideal for getting tube rides.

2.2.4 Reform

A reform happens when a breaking wave starts to fade into deeper water and then forms back into a new breaking wave closer to the shore.

For example: a big wave may be breaking in a dumping/close out situation and it then travels into deep water. At this point, the breaking wave stops breaking. Then, as it travels in and hits a sandbank or underwater formation, it will start to break again. The wave is said to have "reformed".

The wave can reform into good left or right hand breaks.

2.2.5 Step

A step occurs when a wave forms within a wave creating an extra drop in the wave face. Steps in the wave usually occur over reef or rock surfaces but can also occur over sandbanks especially where there are fast running currents and rips.

As the wave moves across submerged formations (reef, rocks, sandbanks), the wave can suck back over that formation. As the wave stands up, it creates another wave below the original wave. This looks like a step. Steps can be any size.

Look out for steps when riding a wave. They can form up in front of you. The best way to handle the wave with steps is to angle across and down the step as soon as possible, before the step builds up too much.

Before entering the water, you can check to see if steps are occurring and at which places on the waves. That way, you are aware and prepared to handle them.

2.2.6 Double Up

A double up will occur when one wave, travelling to the shore, catches up to another wave. When this happens, the wave you are riding on increases in size to incorporate both waves. Double ups can happen at any time, especially with uneven swell conditions.

The affect on the wave you are riding could be either good or bad. It could cause the wall of your wave to build up providing more drop for you and therefore more speed. Or the double-up can cause the wave to get too large and close-out.

When riding on the wave, you will be able to see if your wave is catching up to another wave. Try to turn down the wave in front of you and into the new drop (the double up). Some surfers use a hopping technique to perform this manoeuvre.

Wave behind   Wave in front

In this photo, the wave behind has caught the wave in front. The wave is about to double up.

3. Wave Direction

Wave direction refers to the direction the wave is breaking when you are looking from the surf back to the shore.

The breaking wave will be described as a "left" hand wave or "right" hand wave. In some instances, the wave can break both "left" and "right" at the same time. You then have the choice of going either "left" or "right".

It could get a little confusing determining if the wave is left or right, when you are standing on the shore looking out at the waves. This is because the wave direction is reversed to when you are in the water.

3.1 Left Hand Wave
As you look from the shore, the wave breaks to the right.

3.2 Right Hand Wave
As you look from the shore, the wave breaks to the left.

3.3 Choice of Left or Right Hand Wave
As you look from the shore, the wave breaks both ways.

4. Wave Frequency

Once you have checked out the wave form and conditions, you will be keen to know how often the waves will be rolling in. That is, how long you will have to wait in the water for the opportunity to catch a wave.

Waves usually come in sets. A set is a group of waves. There are often 3 to 5 waves in a set but this can vary. The first wave is usually smaller with the last wave usually the largest.

There are usually lulls between sets. A lull is a period of no waves in between sets and can continue for anywhere up to 10 minutes or more. Lulls are great for padding out.

In this photo, the waves are coming in. The surfers wait for a lull before entering the water to paddle out to the break.

The lull occurs and now the surfers enter the water to paddle out easily. They retain energy to use surfing the waves.

CHAPTER 4
Select a Suitable Surfing Location

Outcomes

☐ Determine the criteria affecting the selection of a suitable surfing location.
☐ Select a surfing location after considering the factors that affect surfing.
☐ Select a surfing location after considering all statutory and organisational procedures.
☐ Ensure sufficient food and water is available to maintain body well-being during activity.

Selecting the most suitable surfing location to surf on any given day takes a great deal of skill. You will analyse the whole range of factors we have talked about so far.

When deciding to go surfing, here are the types of questions you should be thinking about:

1. Weather conditions - are there any low pressure systems creating swell? Will the weather stay the same or is a weather change expected soon?

2. What are the tides like at the time you want to go surfing? Are the waves closing out? If so, the tide may be low and the waves may be better at a higher tide.

3. What is the wind direction and speed? Is it ideal or will it change to make the surf better or worse?

4. Which surf break will you be surfing at? Will the waves be breaking there?

5. The condition and quality of the water – e.g. glassy, choppy?

6. What is the wave form like? Good? Bad? Ugly?

7. Are there any other wave conditions affecting the waves? Sucky? Steps? Double-ups?, etc?

8. How often are the sets coming in? The waves can be coming in regularly or they may only be coming in sets once every while. Will you have to wait a long time between sets?

9. What is the swell like – small or large?   Are there consistent waves (ground swell) or uneven lines?

10. Are there any water hazards that would not make surfing ideal? e.g. pollution, coconuts, sea creatures?

11. Are there any council/city regulations determining whether you can surf the break (closed beach, private property, designated locations for surfing)?

12. Number of people already out surfing e.g. there may only be one break but it is "crowded". This may affect your ability to catch waves.

13. Your surfing ability. Are the conditions appropriate to your level of skill?

In order to work out the most suitable surfing location, experienced surfers spend time on the shore assessing the above factors. All of these factors will influence your decision on whether there are waves that suit you.

Your ability to assess the above will increase the more familiar you are with the surf location and local weather conditions. The more time you spend following the weather and spending time watching the surf, the better you will be at predicting when to go surfing and the surf conditions that suit you best.

Remember to take adequate food and water if you are surfing. This is important if you are surfing at remote surf locations or in national parks that do not have water and food facilities.

Let's now have a look at some surf locations and analyse the surf conditions on the day to see whether you would go surfing.

Surf Study 1 - Analyse
Surf Conditions

The weather conditions are nice and sunny. The wave form is good but the frequency is inconsistent. The waves are small plus there is a large crowd of people in the water. The tide is dropping so the waves will probably not get better. As this is a reef break, and the tide is low, you will have to walk over some sharp reef.

Summary:

Weather conditions:	The weather is sunny and hot. There are no expected changes in the weather.
Tides:	The tide is low and by checking the tide watch/chart, the tide is going lower.
Wind direction and speed:	There is a light off-shore wind.
Type of surf break:	Reef break.
Condition and quality of the waves:	Glassy. Wave form is quite good although the waves are small.
Other wave conditions:	None.
How often the sets are coming in:	Sets are irregular. No larger wave sets are coming in. Moderate wait in between sets.
What is the swell like:	Ground swell. Consistent form with intervals of 4 to 6 minutes between sets.
Water hazards:	No pollution. No sea creatures. Reef.
Council/city regulations:	None.
Number of people surfing:	Very crowded. Approximately 35 - 40 people.

Surf Study 2 - Analyse
Surf Conditions

On this day, there is a strong cross-shore wind blowing. Overall the wave conditions are not good. Even though the sets are consistent, the waves do not have especially good form. You might get a good ride if you are lucky. The water and air temperatures are warm so being in the water will not be too unpleasant.

Summary:

Weather conditions:	Overcast day. Warm tropical water and air temperature. Rain has been predicted for the day.
Tides:	The tide is high and running out.
Wind direction and speed:	Strong cross-shore wind blowing.
Type of surf break:	Reef break (rock platform).
Condition and quality of the waves:	Waves are about 3 to 4 ft. Uneven and lumpy. Crumbling a little bit at the top and sectioning out.
Other wave conditions:	None.
How often the sets are coming in:	Sets fairly consistent.
What is the swell like:	Ground swell.
Water hazards:	Submerged rocks. Some coconuts and tree branches are in the water.
Council/city regulations:	None.
Number of people surfing:	Not crowded. 3 to 4 people.

Surf Study 3 - Analyse
Surf Conditions

Waves are a decent size, good form and consistent. There is a small to medium crowd of people but with the consistency of waves, there is no problem getting waves. You can see that some people are catching nice waves. Even the occasional tube ride is possible. Intermediate to advanced level surfing conditions.

Summary:

Weather conditions:	Overcast. Weather has been stormy but is clear with slight rain. Doesn't look like the weather will get worse.
Tides:	Mid tide going to high tide. At this particular break, the waves should continue to improve perhaps building slightly in size with the incoming tide - pushing the swell in.
Wind direction and speed:	Light to moderate off-shore.
Type of surf break:	Beach break.
Condition and quality of the waves:	Good form. Waves not closing out. Slight chop on the face of the outside waves. The inside waves seem to be cleaner (less chop).
Other wave conditions:	Hollow waves - making for good tube rides.
How often the sets are coming in:	Regular.
What is the swell like:	Ground swell.
Water hazards:	None
Council/city regulations:	None
Number of people surfing:	Medium sized crowd.

<h1 style="text-align:center">CHAPTER 5</h1>
<h2 style="text-align:center">The Surfboard</h2>

Outcomes

- ☐ Select the surfboard after consideration of all factors that affect surfing.
- ☐ Check and adjust surfboard (where applicable) and ensure suitability for personal requirements and the surf conditions.

1. Surfboard Shape

Your surfboard is the most important aid in surfing. It can dramatically assist your level of surfing skill.

In the *Learn to Surf for Beginners* manual, you became familiar with the basic parts of the surfboard such as the tail, nose, bottom, deck and fins.

Because each person is different, and there are many varied wave conditions, each part of the surfboard can also be shaped in a variety of dimensions, designed to enhance your surfing performance.

You may have heard surfers describing types of boards as:
- 7"2' Rawson gun
- 6"6' rounded pin Channel Island
- 6'4 "swallow tail Webber
- 6'3 area round tail Ripcurl
- 6' 6" pintail Dahlberg
- McTavish traditional old style long board

What surfers are describing here is the length, tail shape and brand. This description provides a snapshot of the board. You may then go on to describe the finer details of the board and in what surf conditions the board rides best.

Each part of the surfboard design has a part to play in:
- manoeuvrability
- speed
- stability
- ability to catch waves

As an intermediate surfer, you are now at a stage where you will be able to choose a board that will help you gain the skills necessary to take you to the advanced level. If you have a board that is not suited to you or the particular wave conditions, then you will not ride the waves as well as you could.

Let's have a look at the different parts of the surfboard so you can get an understanding of what is available and the affect each part of the surfboard has on your ability to ride waves.

The parts of the board we will cover are:
- plan shape (outline)
- length
- thickness
- rocker
- bottom
- tail
- nose
- rails

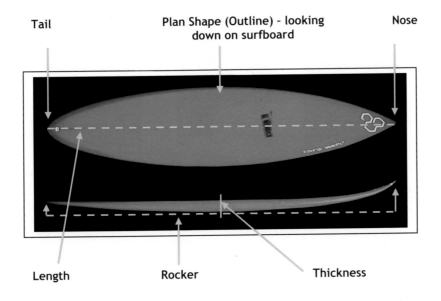

Tail   Plan Shape (Outline) – looking
         down on surfboard   Nose

Length   Rocker   Thickness

1.1 Surfboard Length

The length of the surfboard usually relates to size of the wave you are likely to be surfing. Longer surfboards are generally used for larger waves. Smaller length surfboards are generally used for smaller waves.

The surfboard length helps in your ability to catch waves. The longer surfboard gives you more length to paddle into the wave.

The longer length also allows you to paddle faster. In larger waves, there is a lot of water rushing up the face of the wave as it moves into shore. If you do not paddle fast enough, the wave will quickly pass you by.

Some different board lengths

Short board

Gun

Long board

1.2 Plan Shape (Outline)

This refers to the shape of the overall area of the surfboard. You can describe the plan shape of a surfboard as having a wider shape or a narrower, sharper shape.

The shape affects manoeuvrability and stability. A wider plan shape means the surfboard will turn more freely off its tail. A narrower plan shape means less manoeuvrability on smaller waves. However, the narrower plan shape contributes, with length, to speed and stability in larger waves.

The main plan shapes are:

- Short (small wave board) – a wider board that is pulled in at the nose, with a variety of area tail shapes.

- Gun – (large wave board) - a longer narrower surfboard than a short board with a streamlined nose and tail.

- Long board - also referred to as a Malibu board. Generally wide overall and long, starting from around 9 foot. Long boards are also available in a shorter length and are referred to as mini-mals or fun boards.

Short board (e.g. 6ft 2")

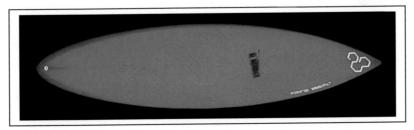

Gun (e.g. 7ft 6")

Long board (Malibu) (e.g. 10ft 4")

1.3 Thickness

Thickness determines how the board will float on the water and its balance (stability). A thicker board can make paddling easier however it may make duck diving through the waves more difficult. A little more thickness can also help you ride better in slow, sluggish waves.

The board's thickness is usually taken from the centre or the thickest part of the board. The tapering of the thickness, from nose to tail, is referred to as the foil.

Thickness can be distributed through surfboards differently. Generally, there is more thickness in the middle of the board where you need flotation for paddling. There is less thickness in the tail and nose. Some surfers may prefer more thickness in the nose and tail depending on their riding styles.

The thickness of a surfboard will vary quite a lot depending on a number of things like the length of the board and the weight of the person. e.g. someone who is tall and weighs 90 kgs (14 stone) will need a surfboard made longer and thicker than a board made for someone who is shorter and of lighter weight.

Surfboard thickness can vary by measurements as little as 1/8th or even 1/16th of an inch. It may not seem very much but through the volume of the board, it will make a difference to your ride.

1.4 Rocker

Rocker is the curve in the board (from nose to tail), when looking from the side angle. Rocker can be very minor or increased to be very pronounced.

The amount of rocker affects speed and manoeuvrability.

Less rocker means the board sits more flatly on the water surface. The board will be faster but have less manoeuvrability.

The more rocker a board has, the slower the board will be but it will have more manoeuvrability. It will be able to pull tight arcs in turns.

You need more rocker in bigger waves. The larger waves mean you are going fast and you want the board to slow down so you are able to turn it.

The difference in thickness and rocker of some surfboards
are shown below.

Short board

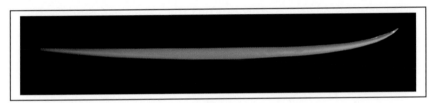

Gun

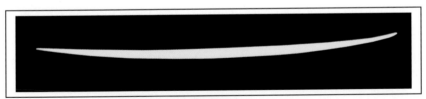

Long board (Malibu)

1.5 Bottom

The bottom of the surfboard is usually flat with designs shaped into it to further enhance surfing performance.

Bottoms can have:
- vee (wedge shaped) throughout the tail
- channels through the tail
- concaves (single, double)

The design on the bottom of the surfboard will affect the speed.

Surfboard with channels

These changes to the bottom of the surfboard direct the flow of water out the back of the board in different ways. This in turn affects your speed. The type of design depends on your personal surfing style and wave conditions.

1.6 Tail

The tail is the most important part of the surfboard. It is the part of the board you turn off and therefore determines manoeuvrability and therefore, performance.

The performance (manoeuvrability) of the board is referred to as how "loose" or "tight" ("stiff") the board is. Generally the more area in the tail (i.e. the wider the tail), the easier the board will turn. This is because there is more surface area in contact with the water.

Turning ability is also affected by the type of fins and their placement on the board. We will discuss more about fins later in this chapter.

In larger surf, you would probably want more stability and therefore have a tail that is tighter (pin tail). In large surf, you are dropping down big waves and moving faster. The narrowness of the tail will also help to hold the fins in the water.

In smaller surf, the water is not moving as fast allowing you to have more control over the board. You may prefer to have more performance (manoeuvrability) and hence have a looser tail shape. e.g. round tail, swallow tail.

The photo's of the different types of tails below rate the looseness of the tail. The fish tail is the loosest with the pin tail being the tightest. With each of these tail shapes, you can also have a wider or narrower tail which will further affect performance (manoeuvrability).

Photo 1 - the most loose
Photo 6 - the least loose.

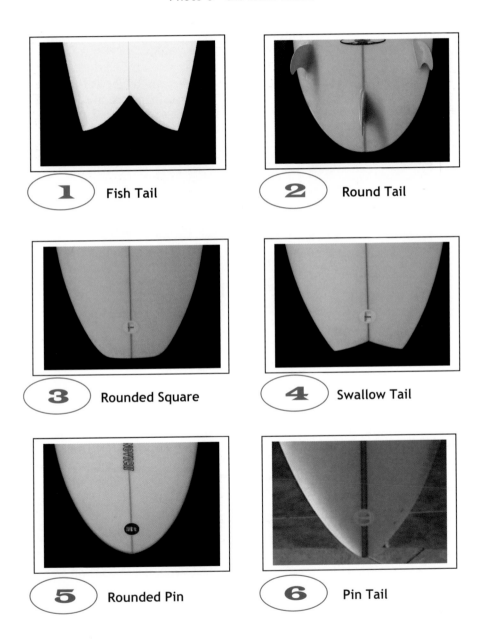

1 Fish Tail

2 Round Tail

3 Rounded Square

4 Swallow Tail

5 Rounded Pin

6 Pin Tail

1.7 Nose

The nose is found at the front quarter section of the surfboard. It is an extension of the board's rocker and is lightly curved up. This curve is commonly referred to as the nose lift.

The shape of the nose on the surfboard helps with speed. The nose shape depends on the surfboard outline. The nose is more pointed, but with more area, on a shorter board and more pointed on a gun.

A full area nose (like a long board/Malibu) allows you to get at the front of the board and trim along the wave. There is more surface area in the water so the board will plane along on the water surface a bit easier than a thinner, narrower, pulled in board.

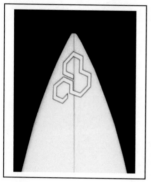
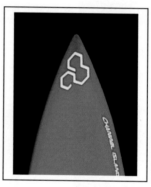

Sharp (area) pulled in nose.
Typical short board

Tapered in nose
(Gun - big wave board)

Full area nose
(Long board /Malibu)

1.8 Rails

The rails are the side edges of the surfboard. Rails help with direction by "cutting" into the wave surface. Rails come in many designs – from slow curving, soft rails to very square (hard, boxy). The rails are always sharper down near the tail to let you hold a true line and to allow the water to release off the tail cleanly.

The harder the rail edges, and the further the edge runs up toward the nose, the more the board will cut into and hold the wave's face. This is more suitable for larger, steeper faces where you are going fast. You want the rails to grip on the wave's face. In smaller waves, the opposite is true. Here you will want soft rails through most of the board to allow you to turn easily, without catching any edges.

Soft
Edge

Hard
Edge

Surf Study - The Surfboard

Let's have a look at all 3 types of surfboards to see how the different parts of the surfboard affect the performance.

Short board (6ft 2")

Small to medium waves. Some stability but with speed and manoeuvrability.

Wider plan shape and tail provides a little more stability and manoeuvrability, but less speed. More rocker makes the board slightly slower but provides more manoeuvrability. More difficult to catch waves with shorter length. However, more thickness helps you paddle into the waves.

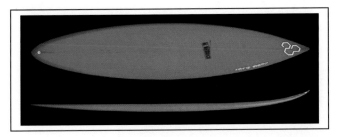

Gun (7ft 6")

Big waves. Some stability, not too loose. With length to catch waves.

A narrower plan shape means less stability. The longer length will help with stability needed to catch big waves. To gain manoeuvrability, there is more rocker. This also helps to slow the board making turning easier on bigger waves.

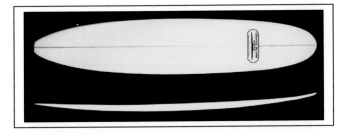

Long board (Malibu) (10ft 4")
Any waves - depending on your ability. Very stable, easy to catch waves.

The width and length make this board very stable. Need to increase performance (manoeuvrability) due to length and heavy weight of board. Therefore, the board needs much more rocker. Short board style tail helps with manoeuvrability. Length makes it easy to catch any size waves.

2. Surfboard Composition

The original surfboards were made from wood (balsa). Today, most surfboards are made from foam and fibre-glass. Surfboarder designers and manufacturers are always looking for better materials and methods of construction and as a result, surfboards are now made from other materials.

2.1 Fibre-glass Boards

These surfboards are the most popular as they are light weight, easy to ride, easy to make and repair. The fibre-glass board is made from polyurethane or what is generally called "foam" with a stringer, fibre-glass and resin. The surfboard maker shapes foam blanks into the desired shapes.

The foam blank has a stringer down the middle. The stringer gives the surfboard strength and helps to stop it from breaking. The stringer is made from timber. Older style surfboards often had more than one stringer. Stringers can also come in different thicknesses with the thicker stringers weighing more.

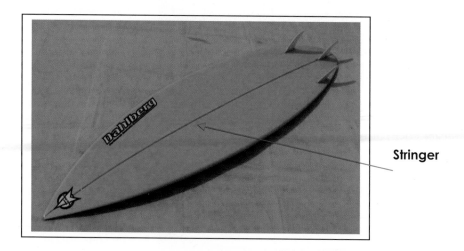

Stringer

Fibre-glass matting (or glass) is then layered over the foam. Fibre-glass, when combined with resin, helps protect the shaped foam from damage. Resin is the liquid substance applied to the fibre-glass that hardens to give the surfboard its smooth finish. Fibre-glass can be applied in different thicknesses (e.g. 2, 4, 6 ounces) to different areas of the board. An extra layer or thicker fibre-glass matting applied to the deck down near the tail will give extra strength where your knee/foot goes when duck-diving. The thinner the layer of fibre-glass, the lighter the board will be however it also means the board will be prone to deform and break more easily.

Surfboard colour/design, or what is commonly called, "the spray" is applied to the surfboard after shaping, onto the foam, and before glassing. A spray can be plain/simple to very intricate/complex - virtually anything you want is possible.

2.2 Other Board Composition

More recent developments have seen the introduction of surfboards made from epoxy resin in combination with other materials. These boards can be more buoyant, lighter and stronger. One drawback is that they can be difficult to repair.

Other surfboard compositions include:

- epoxy with polystyrene foam core, PVC layers bonded by fibre-glass
- wood veneer
- soft tops - hard epoxy board with EVA rubber deck and rails
- bamboo
- foam

Epoxy resin board. Notice there is no stringer.

3. Fins

Fins are found on the bottom of the board near the tail. The main purpose of fins is to give the board direction and help you hold a line on the wave. If you didn't have fins, you would have very little control and would tend to slip sideways and spin around.

Over the years there has been much experimenting with the number of fins, shape, fin attachment systems and fin material and design in order to find fins that will provide the best holding power, drive and flexibility. There is a wide variety of fin style shapes and sizes available. As surfing technology continues to develop, new fin materials and shapes are constantly being brought to the market.

3.1 Number of Fins

Surfboards may have up to five fins. The single fin is the oldest style of fin. The board had one large fin in the centre of the tail. These fins had a much wider base. They were much longer therefore creating more drag and having less manoeuvrability.

The invention of the twin fin board allowed riders to have shorter and narrower fins at the base, separated to each side of the board. This meant the tail could be wider and hence give the surfer more manoeuvrability (at times, too much manoeuvrability!).

The introduction of the thruster was like having a stabiliser (the middle fin) at the back of the twin fin. All three fins were changed to be the one smaller size rather than two larger twin fins and one smaller stabiliser. The thruster gave more manoeuvrability to the ride but still had good traction due to the tripod placement of the three fins around the tail. For these reasons, the thruster is now the most popular fin combination.

Single Fin

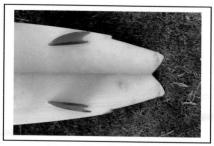

Twin Fin (Two fins)

Thruster (Three fins)

Four fins

3.2 Fin Material and Shape

All fins used to be made from wood and then came fibre-glass. Fibre-glass is still the most commonly used fin material due to its flexing and strength characteristics. The fins are glassed to the board at the time of making the board. Fin designers are also using other materials such as plastic, carbon fibres, carbon ceramics, glassed fibre reinforced nylons.

Fibre-glass Fins

Fins can be curved (raked), angled and have different degrees of flexibility. Fins can also differ in base to tail thickness. Each of these designs causes a different affect from lifting the tail, giving you more speed, reducing drag and flex (the amount of movement in the fin when riding the board).

3.3 Fin Systems

Some boards have removable fins. These are typically called a "fin system" and allow you to change your fins to suit different surf conditions (or complete removal for travelling/storage). The surfboard has specially designed fin attachment systems fitted into board that allow you to place and lock/clip in the fins.

Being able to change your fins allows you to further respond to the specific wave conditions and your own surfing style.

Fins can also be placed in different positions on the tail of the board depending on the type of fin attachment system fitted to the board.

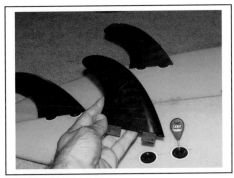

Some other types of fins/fin systems are shown below:

Fibre-glass fins. Attached to the board at two points only.

Plastic composite fins. Attached to the board at front part of fin only.

Fins that swivel to allow you to adjust angle.

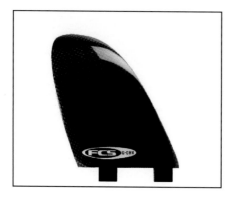

Curved fin

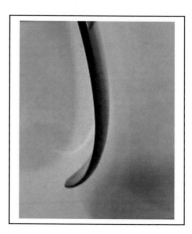

4. Surfboard Damage

Because surfboards are made from foam and fibre-glass, they are susceptible to damage. Always check your surfboard for damage.

Look for:
- Fractures - small cracks in the glass
- Dings - where the glass is broken and water leaks into the foam
- Broken board – any part of the board that is broken (usually nose or centre)
- Yellowing – from leaving your board in direct sunlight over a long period

If any damage occurs, it is best to repair these as soon as possible. If you leave it, water will seep in and the board will get waterlogged. The fibre-glass matting might also start to delaminate (separate) from the foam. Some small fractures will not allow water seepage therefore do not need repairing. Larger fractures, if leaking, will need repair. Never leave your board in the back of the car in the sun. It can delaminate.

Also check your fins for damage. Look for:
- Broken fins – completely cut off from the board
- Cracked fins – small crack in along the sides of your fins (fin wobble)
- Broken or cracking around the fin attachment device

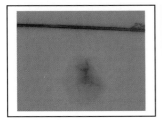 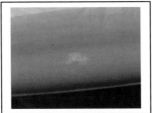 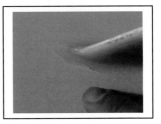

Ding	**Fracture**	**Cracking**
Hole in board that has been repaired.		around fins.

Your local surf shop will generally be able to help you with repairs or be able to recommend who can help you. You can also purchase repair kits and repair the board yourself. We talk more about how to do this in the *Learn to Surf-Advanced Level* manual.

5. Choosing a Surfboard for the Intermediate Surfer

The type of surfboard you choose depends on your weight, surfing conditions and surfing ability.

At the beginner stage you got used to balancing on a longer, wider surfboard. You can now move on to a smaller board so that you can start to perfect your manoeuvres. Usually a short, thin and light weight surfboard is for the more advanced surfer as it will respond much quicker than a longer, wider, heavier board.

The ideal intermediate board would be somewhere between the beginner's board and an advanced board. It could have:

- A slightly smaller overall area (plan shape) than the beginner's board – to give you more manoeuvrability in the water.

- A full round or rounded square tail – easier to turn.

- A full area nose gives you more planing surface in the water (to get over those flat sections).

- The thickness will depend on your weight.

- As a rule of thumb, for the intermediate surfer, the length of the surfboard should be about 4 to 6 inches longer than your height.

As an intermediate surfer, a short to medium size board should suit you. The thickness will be relative to your height and weight. i.e. between 5ft 10 inch to 6ft 6 inches.

If you are a tall person with a heavy build, you should have a slightly longer and thicker surfboard so that the board doesn't stall on you over flat sections. A young grommet may think a 6ft surfboard is a gun. A 5ft board would be more suitable!

At the intermediate level, don't be overly concerned about the thickness of a surfboard. Most boards will have a good foil throughout. If you are thinking of purchasing a new custom board the shaper will always ask you your weight to make you a board that will be of a thickness appropriate to your weight as well as your surfing ability.

CHAPTER 6
Surfing Accessories

Outcomes

☐ Check and adjust surfing accessory equipment (where applicable) and ensure suitability for personal requirements and the conditions.

In addition to the surfboard, other surfing accessories can be used to help you surf.

1. Leg-Ropes (Leashes)

Specially designed cord that connects you to the surfboard. The leg-rope (also known as a leash) is attached to your ankle at one end and into the plug on the board, at the other end.

Before leg-ropes, surfers sometimes had to do a lot of swimming if they fell off their board. The first leg-ropes were dog collars. They were strapped around the ankle, attached to a rope and then tied through a hole drilled through the fin. There have been lots of changes to leg-ropes since those days. The leg-rope you choose to use will depend on the size of your board and the waves you are surfing.

1.1 Parts of the Leg-rope (Leash)

Each part of the leg-rope is designed to make surfing performance better and safer.

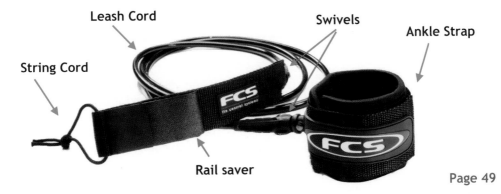

Leash Cord

Swivels

Ankle Strap

String Cord

Rail saver

1.1.1 String Cord

The string cord attaches the leg-rope to the plug in the surfboard. The string cord is attached to the rail saver. Make sure the string cord is tied correctly by having it double reef knotted and as short as possible.

1.1.2 Rail Saver

The rail saver protects the rails from damage. It is a piece of wide material attached by the string cord to the board plug and by the swivel on the leash cord. It sits over the rail of the board. The leg-rope is subject to a lot of strain as it drags through the water. If there were no rail saver, then the leash cord would tear into the rail of the surfboard. As the rail saver is wide, the same cutting effect does not occur as easily.

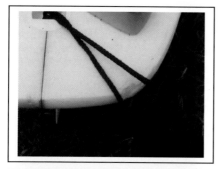

✗ **Incorrect**
Rail saver has not been tied in the correct place. You can see that the string cord is too long and has cut into the rails of the board.

✔ **Correct**
The rail saver should sit over the rails to protect rails from damage.

The rail saver is usually made from polyester and velcro. Some rail savers open up so that you can slip the string cord through the plug and double it up. Rail savers can have a variety of features including different thicknesses, webbing, extra laps to keep from coming undone, extra stiff material to stop rail saver from folding and can be detachable allowing you to change leg-ropes easily.

1.1.3 Leash Cord

The leash cord connects to the rail saver at one end and to the ankle strap at the other end. It is usually made from urethane. Leash cords come in different lengths, thicknesses and therefore differing stretch.

Longer boards need longer leg-ropes. If the leg-rope is too short, you will not be able to move up to the front of the surfboard when doing manoeuvres. Also, if you have to dive off the front of the surfboard, you will not have much room to dive as the surfboard will follow very close behind you.

Also make sure your leg-rope is not too long for the board. If it is too long, the leg-rope will be in the water resulting in unnecessary drag slowing you down. Longer leg-ropes are also usually thicker making them heavier and once again creating more drag in the water.

As the leash cord is made from a stretch material, it recoils. If it was not made from a stretch material, your ankle and leg would be subject to strong hard jerks after a wipe-out.

1.1.4 Ankle Strap

This is the part that wraps around your ankle. It is usually made from polyester/neoprene and Velcro. Ankle straps sometimes have key pockets where you can place your keys.

1.1.5 Swivel

There are usually two swivels – one at each end of the leash cord. One swivel attaches the cord to the ankle strap. Another swivel attaches the cord to the rail saver. Swivels stop the cord from getting twisted and knotty. If you wipe out, you may spin one way and the board spins the other way resulting in the string cord and the leash cord twisting.

1.2 Wearing a Leg-rope (Leash)

Tangling can occur if the leg-rope is not worn properly.

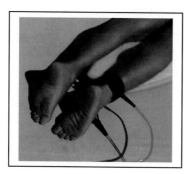

The ankle strap should be worn with the swivel off the side of the ankle and over the side of the surfboard. For a natural footer, this will be off the right ankle and over the right side of the board. For a goofy footer, this will be off the left ankle and over the left side of the board.

If the ankle strap swivel is facing forwards between your feet, when lying on the board, you run the risk of treading on the leg-rope when you stand up.

Also make sure your ankle strap fits snugly around your ankle. If it is too loose, it will flop around and the leash cord might get tangled around your feet.

2. Wax

Wax is applied to the deck of your surfboard to provide traction when paddling or standing.

There are many waxes available to suit different weather and water conditions from hot temperatures to cold temperatures. Check out the manufacturer's label and then experiment with a few different wax brands. Aside from the temperature requirements, your choice of wax will be a matter of personal preference.

You may not need to wax up every session. Use a wax comb so your wax doesn't build up too thick. The thicker the wax, the heavier your board will be.
It is a good idea to take a wax comb out in the water. You may find that your wax becomes too smooth (no traction). If you have a wax comb out in the water, you can save a trip back into shore. You can get small wax combs that can be kept on a string in your boardshorts pocket or even attach one to your leg-rope on a key ring holder.

Remember to keep your wax out of the sun as it will melt. You can store wax in a plastic bag or you can buy special little containers to hold the wax.

3. Traction Pads / Grip

Traction pads are also known as grip and are an alternative to using wax. Their primary purpose is to stop you slipping off the board. They are usually made from EVA foam and can have grooves and steps to help with maximum traction. The different traction pads/grip include:

1. Tail pads. Are placed on the tail of the board. There are many different designs including: kick tails (lifts up high at the back to stops your foot slipping off back of board) and arch bars (designed to arch up under the natural arch of your foot and provides grip right across the base of your foot).

2. Centre deck pads. Are placed around the middle of the board. They can even be placed further up the deck on longer boards.

3. Nose pad - placed on the nose of long boards (Malibu boards).

4. Surfboard Covers

Surfboard covers are used for transporting and storing boards. There are many different surfboard designs for you to choose from. The covers can be made from a variety of materials with added features to help you with carrying/storing, shock protection and extra pockets.

Soft board cover

| Single board cover | Double board cover | Multi board cover with wheels |

5. First Aid Kit

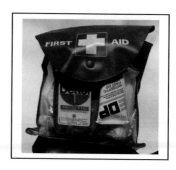

Injuries can occur at any time. The water will can cause small cuts to fester and become infected. A little first aid to any cuts/abrasions can mean you will be able to surf longer and more comfortably.

Make sure you always carry a first aid kit when surfing to remote locations and overseas.

Here's what you should include:
- Tweezers - for pulling out bits of reef / or other sharps things
- Scissors
- Wrap bandage - also use as a tourniquet to cut blood supply to severe injuries
- Sling bandage - for dislocated arm, etc.
- Antiseptic liquids to sterilise and clean the wound - e.g hydrogen peroxide, Betadine, Mercurochrome, Dettol
- Antiseptic drying power - to help the drying and healing process as quickly as possible
- Cotton wool - dabbing a wound clean, putting antispetic on the wound.
- Band-aids - for small scratches and cuts
- Butterfly stitch band-aids - can temporarily pin a large wound that is in need of stitches.

6. Security

These days, most people have car/house keys with them when surfing. Over the years, many ways of keeping your keys with you while you surf have been invented.

Leg-ropes (leashes) and board shorts have special key pockets. A watertight plastic box can also be fitted in your surfboard allowing you to keep your keys and other items with you whilst surfing.

7. Checking Your Equipment

Always check your equipment to ensure it is in good condition: Check for:

- Damage to the surfboard – dings, fractures, broken fibre-glass, etc.
- Damage to fins
- Loose or wobbling fins. They could break out and you could lose a fin. It will cost more to replace the fin rather than repair the fin.
- Nicks or cuts in the leg-rope (so it does not break and you lose your surfboard). These may not look like much but the force of a wave could cause the leg-rope to break at the damaged spot. Even if your leg-rope is in good condition, the force of the wave could be too much for the strength of the leg-rope resulting in the leg-rope breaking. Make sure the thickness of the leg-rope is suitable for the surf conditions.
- The string cord attached between your leg-rope and plug is in good order (so it does not break and you lose your surfboard).
- You have a good cover of wax on the board (so you do not slip off the board whilst riding the waves).
- Make sure the wax is sticky or if you do not have wax, use your wax comb to create a rough and grippy texture.
- Traction pads are firmly attached to the deck.

CHAPTER 7
Surf Clothing

Outcomes

☐ Select personal clothing for the surfing activity and identify the design / construction features that make it appropriate.

1. Surfing in Warm Water Conditions

Surfing in warm conditions is by far the most preferred option by most surfers. Surf clothing requirements are generally very minimal. You have the feeling of being unrestricted in your movement. It is easy to spend hours in the surf as conditions are pleasant. The only surf clothing you really need to surf in warm water conditions is a pair of bathers / boardshorts.

2. Surfing in Cold Water Conditions

Surfing in cold conditions requires much more protection from the elements. The main piece of clothing is the wetsuit and you may also wear booties, hoods and gloves to further protect you from the cold.

2.1 Wetsuits

Wetsuits are used to keep you warm in the ocean. They act as a second layer of skin keeping the body heat between you and the wetsuit. The wetsuit allows a thin layer of water to enter the wetsuit. Your body heat warms up the water and this further helps to keep you warm.

Whilst wetsuits are designed to help keep you warm, they still need to be flexible enough so the surfer can move about comfortably. Technological advances in wetsuit materials and design centre on surfers staying warm in all sorts of weather conditions and having maximum flexibility.

Wetsuits come in varying constructions and materials depending on how cold the water is and the degree of flexibility required by the surfer. You can purchase standard size wetsuits or have a custom made wetsuit made especially for you.

2.1.1 Design

Wetsuits are designed to cover the body. The more body coverage, the warmer you will be in the water. There are different designs of wetsuits.

The most popular are:
- **steamer (or full suit)** is used in extreme cold to cold water conditions.
- **spring suit (or three quarter length)** is generally used in cool to mild temperatures.
- **vests** for mild to warm temperatures. The water may be warm however there may be a cool wind blowing.

You can also get variations on the above including:
- steamer with short arms and long legs
- a long john (steamer with no arms and long legs)
- a short john (short legs and no arms)

The wetsuit you wear will depend on your personal preference.

Wetsuits, with long legs, also typically have knee pads to help protect your knees rubbing against the hard surface of the board and to protect your board from bangs and knocks from your knees.

The wetsuit is made up of panels of neoprene stitched together and usually has a zip, at the back, to allow you to get in and out of the wetsuit. The more panels in a wetsuit, the more flexible the wetsuit will be.

Steamer (Full Suit)
Long sleeves and long legs.

Short Arm Steamer (Full Suit) Short sleeves and long legs.

Long John
No sleeves. Long legs.

Spring Suit
Short sleeves, short legs.

Short John
Short legs, no arms.

Vest - Long sleeves.

Vest - Short sleeves.

2.1.2 Material

Wetsuits are made from a flexible rubber material called neoprene. Neoprene allows the wetsuit to stretch and fit close to your body.

Wetsuits also have a lining on the inside which further helps to retain your body heat. This is called "single line neoprene" and is referred to as a "smoothie" wetsuit. This is because the outside neoprene is smooth rubber.

Wetsuits cans also have a lining on the outside. This is called "double lined neoprene". This extra lining helps protect the wetsuit making it last longer.

Double lined neoprene wetsuits have a material-like look. However, "double lined neoprene" is slightly less flexible and less warmer than the "single lined neoprene" wetsuit.

Lining material is typically made of nylon. Recent advances in wetsuit lining materials include linings made from:
- polypropylene - repels water and helps keep you drier.
- titanium oxide – reflects heat that is radiated from the body. It is generally applied between the neoprene and nylon lining.

Some wetsuits also have extra inserts which provide even more warmth without providing much more thickness.

The more flexible and the less weight the wetsuit can be, the more natural it is to free surfing. Neoprene comes in different quality with the lower quality neoprene not as durable and not as flexible. Neoprene is constantly being improved to ensure the wetsuit is lighter and more stretchy (flexible).

The wetsuit can also have more stretchy material in places that need more flexibility. For example, more flexibility would be useful in the arm, underarm, shoulder panels and lower back especially when paddling and for easier turning.

Wetsuits are generally black in colour. That's because the colour black absorbs heat from the sun more than other colours.

2.1.3 Seams

The seams are the places where water is able to penetrate the wetsuit. When you are moving about in the surf, cold water will be flowing into the wetsuit. The amount of water flowing into, and out of, the wetsuit will determine how warm you will be. That is, how effectively your body can heat up the layer of water that gets into the wetsuit.

The way a wetsuit is sealed at the seams will affect how much water flows into the wetsuit. The less water that enters and exists the suit, the warmer you will be. The seams of the wetsuit can be sealed in different ways including:

Overlock – the least expensive type of stitching. Not watertight. It sticks out and can cause rash.

Flatlock –. flatter stitch than overlock so will not cause as much rash (if any). Not watertight. Not as durable as overlock stitch.

Blindstitch - a flat stitch meaning little rash problems. Stitch does not go through the neoprene. This means there are less holes to let in water. Can also have double blindstitch where the stitching is on both sides. This means there are no holes at all in the neoprene. Less durable than flatlock and overlock stitch.

Glued - applied to blindstitch and double blindstitch seams. The glue helps to further seal the seams.

Protective tape - applied to blindstitch and double blindstitched seams with glue. The tape is applied on the inside seams and provides more smoothness and added sealing. These wetsuits are watertight allowing warm water near the body to stay close to your skin instead of flowing out of the suit as you move in the water. Some wetsuits may have the tape applied on some seams only meaning more water will flow into and out of the suit than a fully sealed suit.

Liquid seal - tape that is rubber welded. This type of seal sits much flatter than protective tape and is very watertight.

Other methods of sealing seams are always being invented.

Flatlock stitch

Tape over part of seam

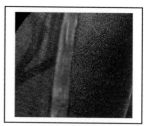
Liquid Seal

Water is also able to enter the wetsuit around the arms, legs and neck areas. The end of the arms and legs of the wetsuit should be tight fitting so as not to let in water.

The neck area of wetsuits generally has an adjustable Velcro fasting. As necks are different sizes, you are able to fasten the Velcro to suit your neck size to fit tightly but not to tight.

Water can also enter through the zip of the wetsuit. Zips come in different qualities from plastic (not so durable) to metal zippers (more durable). Flaps of neoprene (or other material) behind the zip are often in place to help prevent water entering. There can also be larger pieces of material fixed across the back and covering the whole zip area. These are quite effective in reducing water inflow. New advances in wetsuit design have seen zips placed in the shoulder and zipper free wetsuits have also been designed.

2.1.4 Thickness

The thickness of the wetsuit material (neoprene) may vary depending on the temperature of the water. The thicker the wetsuit material, the warmer it will be. However, the wetsuit will not be as flexible.

There are different thicknesses for different parts of the body. The torso of the wetsuit is usually thicker as it is the part that is most exposed to the cool winds. The arms, legs and joints are usually less thick to ensure maximum flexibility.

Wetsuit thicknesses are measured in millimetres. When describing wetsuit thickness, two measurements are usually given. For example, the wetsuit may be described as a 3/2. The first number (usually the largest) is the body torso (back and chest) thickness. The second number (usually the smaller figure) is the arm, leg and joints thickness.

Standard wetsuit thicknesses are:
- 5/4 - very cold water
- 4/3 - cold water
- 3/2 – cool water

You can also get different thicknesses usually with a custom made wetsuit.

2.1.5   Wearing a Wetsuit

Make sure the wetsuit fits tightly but not so tightly that it is uncomfortable. If it is too loose, extra water will stay trapped in the wetsuit making it much heavier.

When you buy a new wetsuit, it can be a little bit tighter. A new wetsuit will loosen up a little after you get out in the water a few times.

Getting into a steamer (full suit) can be difficult at the best of times. Put a plastic bag around your feet and hands and then pull on the wetsuit. You will find that much easier to put on the wetsuit.

2.1.6 Wetsuit Care and Maintenance

As the wetsuit gets older, the neoprene deteriorates. Cracks and tears can develop and the neoprene can stiffen. Seams can also become worn and open.

You can look after your wetsuit by:
- Washing it in fresh water after use.
- Do not put in a spin dryer / washing machine.
- Do not iron.
- Do not leave near heater/fire or on heaters.
- Do not leave in direct sunlight to dry.

Special wetsuit bags help carry/store wet or dry wetsuits.

2.2 Booties

Booties are worn to keep your feet warm. They are made from neoprene with added rubber soles and Velcro sealing around the ankle. The quality of neoprene can also vary from less flexible to more flexible.

The bootie fits above your ankle allowing the long legs of your wetsuit to fit over the booties. This helps to prevent water getting into your booties.

There are many different styles of booties with different toe configurations such as split toe, hidden split toe, mid toe and round toe booties.

Thicknesses can also vary from 1.5mm to 5 mm.

Your choice of booties will depend on how cold conditions are and your personal preference.

2.3 Gloves

Gloves are worn to keep your hands warm. They are made from neoprene and come in different qualities (flexibility) and thicknesses. Gloves usually have individual fingers but sometimes are a mitten design.

2.4 Hoods

Hoods are designed to keep your head warm. They are made from neoprene and also come in various styles and thicknesses. Your choice of hood will depend on your personal preference.

3. Surfing Safety Clothing

This is clothing designed to protect you from the elements.

3.1 Boardshorts

Boardshorts ("boardies") help stop you getting rash on your inner thigh from the board and wax. They are generally worn in warm weather conditions over bathers. Boardies come in all shapes, colours and materials. As you are spending a lot of time in the water, boardies are designed to be comfortable, without rubbing, and to be durable, without falling to pieces (salt water can cause material and stitching to deteriorate).

Design features include soft seams or no seams, softer, flexible material, comfortable waistbands, different waist fastenings and lengths.

3.2 Rash Vest

A rash vest is primarily designed to stop you from getting rash on your neck and underarms, from a wetsuit. It is worn underneath the wetsuit.

Rash can also occur when you are lying on your surfboard, you can get rash on your chest and stomach, from rubbing against the wax on the board.

In both of these cases wearing a rash vest on its own, or underneath a wetsuit, will help prevent rash.

Surfers also wear rash vests for other reasons:
- When surfing in hot sunny conditions, the rash vest be can used to keep the sun off and protect against sunburn.
- For warmth. It may be cooler weather but not cool enough to wear a wetsuit. In this case, the rash vest will provide some protection against the wind. When it is worn underneath a wetsuit, it will also provide more warmth.

Not all surfers wear rash vests underneath their wetsuits or on sunny days to prevent sunburn. It just depends on the type of wetsuit you are wearing, how susceptible you are to developing rash and whether you feel the cold or not.

Rash vests are typically made from lycra. Lycra material is stretchy and wears well in the water. Rash vests can also be made from titanium, and other materials, providing even extra warmth.

The most common type of rash vest warn by surfers is short sleeved. You can also get long sleeve rash vests.

When wearing a rash vest, make sure it fits close to the skin but is not too tight. If the rash vest is too loose, it can cause water to get underneath it, making it heavier. Some surfers may prefer a loose fitting rash vest. Once again, it just depends on your personal preference.

Always check the manufacturer's instructions on how to care and look after your rash vest. These are generally the same as for caring for your wetsuit. Always remember to rinse in fresh water after surfing.

3.3 Booties

Surfers often wear booties, to protect their feet, when surfing over coral or rocky reefs. These booties are different to cold water booties. They are made from neoprene and are usually no more than 2mm in thickness. The neoprene can vary in flexibility. Styles can also vary with different toe styles and extra protection where it is needed.

3.4 Helmets

Helmets can be worn in many different surf conditions. They are used to protect your head against injury from your own surfboard or other people's surfboard.

When surfing over reef, helmets protect your head from damage caused by sharp coral or rocky reefs.

Helmets are made from hard, durable plastic and have added features including shatter proof visor, water proof lining and adjustable audio vents.

3.5 Surf Caps

Surf caps can be worn in the water when surfing. They are designed to keep the sun off your face and protect you from sunburn. They also assist in keeping the sun's glare out of your eyes. They are made from lightweight water resistant and/or flexible materials. Some have mesh on the sides of the hat to let water through.

4. Surfing Assistance Clothing

This is clothing that helps you surf better.

4.1 Webbed Gloves

Webbed gloves are worn to help you paddle more effectively. They have a rubber web skin between each finger. The more surface area you have with your hands, the more water you can pull through and the faster you will paddle. Webbed gloves are made from light weight neoprene and designs include full fingers or mitt gloves without the finger tips.

CHAPTER 8
Enter and Exit the Water

Outcomes

☐ Select a suitable location for entering the water, based on prevailing surfing conditions, council regulations and marked beach zones.
☐ Carry the surfboard out to a depth where it can be safely sat/laid upon, avoiding all surf hazards.
☐ Demonstrate various paddling techniques through broken and unbroken waves.
☐ Demonstrate various methods for paddling out in a safe manner.

1. Enter the Water

If you have decided that you are going out surfing, the next thing to decide is where you will enter the water. You want to choose a place that will allow you to get out to the waves in the quickest way, with the least effort possible.

Before going into the surf, you should be assessing the following to determine where you will enter the water:

1. rips that are present and suitable for use
2. size of the waves
3. frequency of waves and any lulls
4. places to jump off rocks/reef/headlands

If you are unsure of the location, it is a good idea to spend some time observing where the waves are breaking and where other people are <u>entering</u> and <u>exiting</u> the water.

1.1 Rips that are Present and Suitable for Use

Rips are potentially dangerous as they can carry you out to sea. If you get caught in a rip, it could be difficult and tiring to get out of it.

In the *Learn to Surf for Beginners* instruction manual, beginners were advised to stay well away from rips. However, at the Intermediate level, you are now in a position to use the rips to your advantage.

1.1.1 How Rips Form

We talked about rips in the *Learn to Surfer for Beginners* instruction manual. Rips form when water pushed into the shore, is forced to return back out to sea. When the water reaches the shore, it has nowhere to go but back out to sea. A river like flow (current) of water is created. This is called a rip. The flow of the water depends on how much water is hitting the shore (i.e. the size of the waves). Generally, the more water coming in, the faster the rip.

As this water is faster moving, it generally creates a deeper water passage where it is flowing. This is the called a channel. Because the water in the rip is deeper, waves tend not form in this area.

1.1.2 Identifying Rips

You can identify a rip by:
- Water moving out to sea
- A rippled appearance on the surface of the water, when the water around is generally calm.
- Discoloured water due to sand being stirred up from the ocean bottom.
- Foam, bubbles or debris on the surface of the water, moving out to sea.
- Waves breaking on one or both sides of the rip.

Rip

1.1.3 How Surfers Use Rips

Surfers use rips to conserve energy. Paddling out to waves and negotiating broken waves requires a lot of energy. You can conserve energy by paddling as little as possible and by negotiating as few broken or dumping waves as possible.

A rip provides a way to get out to the waves, allowing you to paddle less. When you paddle with a rip, you will generally be carried out to sea with it. The strength of the rip will determine how much you will have to paddle. If it is a very strong rip, you may not need to paddle at all except for some final positioning.

Also, as waves do not break over a rip, you can conserve energy by not having to negotiate any broken or breaking waves.

Rips are most often found at beach breaks. At reef and point breaks any rips present may not always be running in a direction that will assist you. You should carefully assess the rips at each break.

1.1.4 Types of Rips

There are different types of rips. These include rips that:
a) run out from the shoreline to sea
b) run along the shore
c) are present in the line-up
d) run in along the side of a point break

1.1.4 (a) Run Out From the Shoreline to Sea

These are the most useful types of rip as they can carry you out towards your desired location.

Rip

1.1.4 (b)   Running Along the Shore

These rips run along the shoreline and then back out to sea somewhere. These rips can usually be identified by a deep trough of water running along the shoreline (where no waves are breaking). If you come in on a wave, you can get in the rip running across the shoreline and then into the rip running back out to sea. In this situation, this rip will still be useful to you to get back out to the waves.

Rip running along shoreline and then going out to sea. Notice the deeper water along the shoreline and the wave fading out as it approaches the shore.

1.1.4 (c) Present in the Line-Up

In some shore breaks, rips can be present in the line up. Usually, these rips start from the shore and pass through/across the line-up on their way out to sea.

This type of rip will force you to paddle constantly to stay in the correct position.

1.1.4 (d)   Running in Along the Side of a Point Break

The flow of water, in this type of rip, is in the same direction as the waves that are coming in along the point. This type of rip does not assist you in paddling out and will even hinder your progress as they carry you away from your preferred take-off position. You will have to paddle a lot more to stay in position in order to catch waves.

These types of rips are not useful and are not easily identified until you are actually in the water. If there are people in the water surfing, check to see if they are paddling a lot to stay in position. If so, you will know there is a rip. You will be able to gauge how fast the rip is by how much paddling the surfers are doing to stay in position.

Direction of Current

Point Break
The rip is running in the same direction as the incoming waves. The surfers in the water have to paddle constantly just to stay in position.

1.1.5 Choosing Which Rips to Use

Prior to entering the water, you should sit on the shore and spend some time assessing the rips. You will need to assess whether the rip is suitable to use or not. Here are some things to consider when deciding to use a rip:

1.1.5 (a) Location of rips

Where, if any, rips are located. There may be a number of rips present. You can then choose one rip over another depending on which wave area you want to surf.

Sometimes, when you ride a wave in, you may decide to get out onto the shore and walk back to the best place to enter the water. It may be that there is a rip that will help take you out and it is easier to walk to this rip rather than paddle across or against it.

**1.1.5 (b)
Flow of the
rip**

Check the direction the rip is flowing. Is the rip running out and behind the waves or running out in another direction? The rip may be running partly in the direction you want. In this case, <u>use</u> the rip for a little way and then <u>exit</u> by paddling across the rip on a diagonal away from the where the rip is taking you.

A note of caution here is to make sure you exit the rip at the right time so you don't continue to get pulled out to sea or in the wrong direction.

Also make sure the rip is not taking you in front of rocks where waves are also breaking. If this happens, paddle with the rip to quickly pass by the immediate danger.

If the rip is flowing down past a break (usually a point break), try to enter the water as far up the shoreline/point along the break as possible. So that when you get out you won't have been taken too far down the break and have to paddle back to the peak of the break against the current. Also, try to paddle out wide of the waves to avoid the current pushing in against you.

**1.1.5 (c)
Speed of the
rip**

The speed of the rip will affect how fast you get out to the waves.

More often than not rips will generally be present at most surf locations where the waves are breaking well.

Once a rip or current is identified, you can enter the water at this point and it will quickly take you out to where the waves are breaking. The faster the rip, the less energy you will need to paddle out to the waves. Remember to exit from the rip at the appropriate time.

Remember that rips can be dangerous. Refer to *Learn to Surf for Beginners* manual to learn what to do if you get caught in a rip.

In this photo, the rip is flowing out and away from the waves. You should exit the rip and paddle across to the line-up (following the direction of the yellow arrow).

1.2 Size of the Waves

Generally, the size of the waves will determine how easy it will be for you to enter the water. The smaller the waves, the easier it will be. Bigger waves are more powerful making them more difficult to paddle through. If the wave size is larger, the waves will be pushing more water. Bigger waves can also catch you and force you to be washed up on any reef/rocks that are present.

Higher tides and bigger waves usually mean the rips will be stronger and run faster because there is a far greater volume of water moving around.

1.3 Frequency of Waves and Any Lulls

Observe the water to see how often the sets are coming in and how long the lulls last between sets. Time your entry into the water to coincide with the beginning of a lull. This makes it easier to enter the water and paddle out to where the waves are breaking.

Rips may not always be present or be very weak. In these situations, you will have no choice except to go through, or around, the waves.

1.4 Places to Jump off Rocks/Reef/Headlands

To save you a long and tiresome paddle, you can sometimes jump off rocks/headlands/reef to allow you to, easily and quickly, get out to the break or close to it.

Surf Study - Jumping
Off Rocks/Reef/Headlands

1 Always be careful entering water/waves where you are unfamiliar with the submerged rock formations.

Timing is important. Time your jump into the water just on top of the wave that has come in so that the outward flow of water, as the wave subsides, will help sweep you out into the channel/wave line up.

2 Spring off the rocks just before the wave is about to hit the rocks. This forces the water up under you and your board and also helps you out into the surf by using the wave's natural backwash.

When jumping off rocks, always hold the slack in your leg-rope (leash) so that it does not get tangled around your feet or any rocks.

3 Watch out for freak waves or hidden rocks which may come to the surface as the water sucks out to form the next wave.

1.5 Choosing a Place to Enter the Water

Let's have a look at the different breaks and see which way you can enter the water.

Every surf break is different and can even change on a day to day basis. Try to use common sense and observe what other surfers are doing.

Also check the beach for any council/city regulations that apply to surfing in the area. Some beaches have specially marked places for swimmers and surfers to ensure you only surf in designated areas.

1.5.1 Beach Break

Most beach breaks have rips making it easy to enter the water and get out back to the waves.

Surf Study 1 - Beach Break

At this beach break, the waves are breaking left and right.

There are two rips running out from the beach.   You can use the rips to get out to the waves.

Enter the water at either rip depending on which section of waves you intend riding.

Surf Study 2 - Beach Break

At this beach break, waves are coming in at different places due to the possible presence of sandbanks and the shifting peak of the swells coming in. The rips appear to be very light.

Entry into the surf is best to either side of where the waves are breaking.

1.5.2 Point Break

Surf Study 1 - Point Break

A. Enter Here   **B. Enter Here**

At this point break, the waves are breaking to the right. There are two places where you can enter the water.

One way is to go around at the back of the waves (entry A). This is a longer paddle however there do not appear to be any strong rips or currents.

The other way is to walk up to the point (entry B) and paddle from there out to the waves. The waves are breaking so you will need to paddle through some waves. However the waves are not too large and the distance to paddle is much shorter than at entry A. Also remember to wait for a lull then hit it quickly.

Surf Study 2 - Point Break

Direction of rip

1. Off the rocks

3. Enter from beach

2. Enter from beach at headland

This is a right hand point break. There is a strong current running along the point break in the same direction as the surf.

There are a number of places to enter the water:

1. Jumping off the rocks. There is a great deal of backwash plus a strong current. Only experienced surfers should jump in off these rocks at this break.

2. Off the beach, just inside the rocks at the head of the point. Timing here is important. The surfer should only enter the water when there is a lull in the waves otherwise you can be washed back onto the rocks or washed down along the surf break.

3. Further down the beach where the waves are breaking. This is the easiest place to enter the water. However, the surfer will not be at the start of the break and will have a much longer paddle to reach a desired take-off point.

1.5.3 Bombora Break

Surf Study 1 - Bombora Break

At this bombora break, the surfer has been towed out to the break as the break is a long way from shore.

Getting to this break is by way of jet ski.

Jet ski rider   Surfer on wave

1.5.4 Reef Break

When surfing a reef break, look for any break in the reef formation. That is, deeper water which allows you to paddle through the reef and not be scrapping your fins. Also, check that the break in the reef is not in the way of breaking waves.

Remember to look for rips heading out to sea. This will assist you in getting out to where the waves are breaking in. Walk out across the reef until there is enough water under you to start paddling. Wearing booties will help protect your feet, when walking over sharp coral reefs.

If a break in the reef is not present or you cannot see a place where you can jump off the reef, it will probably be a difficult place to go out and surf. Or, it might mean a long paddle off a beach or bay to get to the waves.

Also check out how you can get back to shore. It may not be so easy to get back to shore over the reef. Check for any breaks in the reef formation that allow you to get in. See how the waves are breaking into the shore and whether you can easily get to breaks in the reef. If there is no break in the reef formation, you may be able to ride a wave in up and on top of the reef.

Surf Study 1 - Reef Break

At this reef break - there is an opening in the reef formation where the surfer can enter the water. There is also a current flowing. The surfer should enter at the gap in the reef and move with the current out around the breaking waves and then back to the surf.

Gap in Reef

Surf Study 2 - Reef Break

At this reef break, there is a lagoon area at low tide which is still deep enough to paddle across. There is a constant current running along and down the reef in the same direction as the waves are breaking. There is no gap in the reef. To get to the waves, you have no choice but to paddle over the reef edge (impact zone).

Timing is important here. Look for the lulls in the sets or when smaller sets are breaking to get out quickly. Try to paddle with the current as much as possible even though it is taking you down the reef and away from the peak of the reef. Paddle on an angle that will get you out and behind the waves (impact zone), into the safer, deeper water.

2. Negotiating Waves

Once you have entered the water, you first have to get past broken and unbroken waves that are between the shore and where you want to catch the waves.

2.1 Negotiating Broken Waves

2.1.1 Duck Dive

The best way to get through waves is to use the "duck dive" method.
The aim of the duck dive is to get you, and the board, beneath the breaking power of the wave and to continue paddling out to where you want to surf. It is similar to the technique a duck uses. (The Japanese call the duck dive the "dolphin through".)

The duck dive relies on timing and speed. That is, the amount of time it takes to push the board under water and pull your body in close to the board so that you and the board slide under the water as one, in a fluid motion. The natural curling motion of the wave, and the buoyancy of your board, pulls you out at the back of the wave.

The duck dive can be performed using either the knee or foot to force the tail of the surfboard underwater. When wanting to duck dive deeply under larger waves, the foot on the tail is often preferred.

When duck diving, it is imperative you avoid the impact zone of the wave. This is where all the force of the wave will come down as it throws over. If you dive too early, you will come up right under the impact zone. If you dive too late, the wave will hit you and knock you around, or even separate you from your board.

A duck dive should be done while the wave is approximately 1 ½ metres (4 ½ feet) from you. Things that can go wrong when duck diving include:
- Not pushing down far enough, you will not clear the wave.
- Not raising your leg – making it more difficult to push the board under water.
- If you use your foot, be careful your foot does not slip off the tail.
- Not timing the duck dive correctly.
- You need to be moving forward when you do the duck-dive. The faster you are paddling, the easier it is to duck dive.
- If your board is thicker (and therefore more buoyant) it will be harder to duck dive. This applies to long boards (Malibu boards). As a result, these surfers often use the eskimo roll or rollover technique that was discussed in the *Learn to Surf for Beginners* manual.

Surf Study - Performing
The Duck Dive

1   Paddle forward towards the wave. About 1 ½ metres (4 ½ feet) before the wave, grab the rails of your board, just below your shoulder height.

2   Force the nose of the board under water and forward in the same action, by extending your arms as if you were doing a push-up. At the same time, hold one knee/foot flat down against the board. The knee/foot applies pressure forcing the back of the board down. Raise the other leg into the air as this will also help push you and the board deeper under water.

3   As soon as the board is submerged under water, quickly pull your body into the board. Continue to keep the one leg raised up off the board. Your knee/foot continues to apply pressure downwards on the board (as the wave rolls over you).

4   By this time, the wave will have rolled over you. Keep your body pulled into the board. The nose will start to rise up toward the surface.

5   You will naturally pop up after the wave has passed and then you can continue paddling out.

Surf Study - Performing
The Duck Dive - In the Ocean

Here's what it looks like in the ocean.

1   Paddle forward towards the wave.

2   About 1 ½ metres (4 ½ feet) before the wave, grab the rails of your board, just below your shoulder height.

3   Force the nose of the board under water and forward in the same action. Hold one knee/foot flat down against the board. Raise the other leg into the air.

4   As soon as the board is submerged under water, quickly pull your body into the board. Continue to keep the one leg raised up off the board.

5   You will naturally pop up after the wave has passed and then you can continue paddling out.

These photos, of the duck dive, are taken underwater. You can see the surfer extending his arms to submerge the board and one knee/foot pressing down on the tail, with the other leg out of the water.

Practice Tips:

Practice duck diving on very small waves.
Practice duck diving in flat water

2.2 Negotiating Unbroken Waves

2.2.1 Paddle Through

When the wave is not standing up too much, you can paddle through the unbroken wave.

For example, the wave may only be 2 ft high but very wide. When paddling up and over this wave, you will get to a point (near the crest of the wave), where your body weight will cause the surfboard to sink into the wave, rather than you going up any more and over. As the wave builds up, it will start to lift up and wash over the nose of your surfboard and may then cover your head. At this point, you run the risk of your body and board being separated by the wave passing over you.

To stop being separated from your board, quickly hold your hands flat to the bottom of the board (i.e. hands placed near the rails or closer to the centre of the board depending on your preference). This action will hold your body and board together. The aim is to maintain the traction so you do not get separated from your board as you pass through the unbroken wave.

It is also important, at this point, to have your mouth shut and blow out lightly through your nose, as the wave passes over your head. This will help you avoid getting a mouth full of water and avoid any water getting forced up your nose.

2.2.2 Using the Duck Dive

If a wave is starting to peak, it may not be safe to paddle over it. By the time you get to the top of the wave, the lip would be beginning to pitch over. The peaking wave could easily throw you down into the impact zone of the wave.

In this situation, you can use the duck dive technique to negotiate through the unbroken waves.

Surf Study - Negotiate
Unbroken Waves - Duck Dive

1   As you are paddling up a medium / larger unbroken wave face, you will get to a point where the nose of your board will begin to sink into the wave face.

2   At this stage, you should do a duck dive through the wave.

The duck dive will force your board and body into the wave.

3   Perform the duck dive the same way as you would when doing a duck dive in front of a broken wave.

As the wave passes over, you will naturally float up out the back of the wave.

3. Paddling Out

3.1 Paddling Past a Surfer Riding a Wave

When paddling out, the correct thing to do is to paddle to the inside, of the surfer riding the wave, and towards the broken part of the wave. This is done so you do not interfere with the rider. Alternatively, it is better to be wide enough of the surfer on the wave, to paddle up over the wall or clean face of the wave.

✔ **Correct**
Paddle to the inside, towards the broken part of the wave.

✘ **Incorrect**
The paddling surfer should be paddling straight towards the surfer riding the wave. The surfer riding will have passed by and the paddler will not have interfered with the surfer.

If you find that a surfer is moving fast on a wave and heading towards you as you paddle out, the correct thing to do is to stop paddling in the water and let the surfer manoeuvre around you - either in front or behind you. If you keep paddling forwards, the surfer may have already decided to turn up in front of you and could end up running over you. You will be at fault here.

3.2 Surfing Past People Paddling Out

If you are surfing on a wave and there are surfers paddling all around you, you need to make judgments as to which people you can surf above and which you can go down and around. This especially applies in crowded conditions.

If you are uncertain whether you can get around the people, turn up and off the wave. Or, you could drop down and right around, behind the paddlers. Your ability to surf around paddlers also depends on the number of people and how they are spaced. It is a matter of personal judgment as all situations are different.

Surfer is heading towards paddler.

Paddler remains calm and stops still in water. Surfer turns to avoid a collision with paddler.

4. Getting Out of the Water

The easiest way for you to get back to the shore is to catch a wave in. You may be able to ride it most of the way into the shore and some experienced surfers can surf a wave right up to the shore break.

You may surf the wave standing up and then the wave starts to fade. At this point, you can lie down on the board and glide into the shore. The best place to put your hands is on the nose of the board, allowing you to easily balance and guide the board into the shore.

Make sure you do not head into rips when heading into the shore. You can use up all your energy and get no-where. Rips can also take you back out to sea.

Once you get near the shore, never walk straight out of the water without checking to see what the waves are doing behind you. Some waves can double up on the shore resulting in you being wiped out heavily.

4.1 Getting out of the Water at a Reef Break

Getting out of the water at a reef break can be tricky especially if there are no gaps in the reef. You may have no option but to ride a wave in up and on top of the reef.

As the wave is breaking in, try to get in just behind on the white water so you are not pushed onto the reef. You should still have the momentum of the wave. So, when the wave hits the reef, you are lifted up, on top of the reef, with the wave. Then you have to grapple onto the reef so you don't get sucked back into the water or across the reef as the wave rushes off the reef.

As you feel the wave diminish over the reef, slide off the side of your board and then walk the rest of the way to the shore. Booties are best worn in these situations.

The water may be so shallow that your fins scrape on the reef. In this case, you can turn your surfboard upside down and walk along side it instead of having to carry the board. You can also use the board to take a bit of weight off your feet as you walk in.

Be careful as reef may be sharp on your feet/hands. Reefs often have deep pot holes that you cannot see because of the swirling water. You could step into these and hurt your leg/s. Be careful. If in doubt, wait until you can see the bottom of the reef before moving then move very carefully and watch your step.

CHAPTER 9
Surfing Skills

Outcomes

☐ Select appropriate waves to catch and ride.
☐ Demonstrate awareness of other persons in the vicinity and apply surf etiquette when riding waves.
☐ Demonstrate the ability to control the surfboard in a wipe-out, ensuring personal safety and with regard for the safety of other surfers.

1. Waiting for Waves

Now that you have entered the water, you are in a position to catch a wave. The first thing you will do is wait for the right wave to come.

You can either lie down or sit on the surfboard whilst waiting for the waves.

1.1 Sitting on the Surfboard

Sitting up on the surfboard gives you an elevated position so that you can see the waves approaching. If the swells are big, then this is not as important, as no matter how high you sit on the board, you will not be able to see past the waves in front of you.

Sitting up on the surfboard may also help in stopping you from being dragged away, especially if a strong current is present. Your legs and body also act a bit like an anchor assisting you to stay in position.

When sitting on the surfboard, make sure the nose of the surfboard is just out of the water. If the nose of the board is under the water, the passing swell can cause you to be put off balance by dragging your surfboard sideways or under water.

1.2 Lying Down on the Surfboard

You may also choose to lie down on the surfboard whilst waiting for waves. Lying on the board allows you to quickly paddle into position as the waves approach. However, it may mean that you cannot easily see the waves coming as well as if you were sitting up on your board. If you are lying on the board, you may occasionally sit up at the crest of waves to check and see what waves are coming in.

If a strong current is present, you may have no option but to lie on the surfboard so that you can continue to paddle against the current and maintain your position in the surf line up.

Sitting up or lying down on the board is a matter of personal choice. If you have been lying down paddling, you may like a change and sit up for a rest and stretch. Alternatively, you may like to just stay lying down to rest.

2. Choose the Waves to Ride

Choosing waves to catch is a difficult skill to master. You will be assessing the swell as it comes in, noting where it is peaking, but not shouldering too much and/or closing out. Too much shoulder (wall) might mean the wave will close out. Or, a section may close out down the line a bit before it gets to the shore. So, watch the waves carefully and note how and where the waves are breaking. Also take note of any special characteristics.

2.1 Choose Wave Direction

Before catching the wave, you will usually have decided which direction you are going to be surfing on that wave. That is, whether you will be going right or left. On most beach break waves, you can go either right or left. The wave may build up in a wedged shape allowing you to choose either a left or right hand wave to surf.

Usually, you will have decided prior to entering the water which direction you will be surfing – based on wave conditions and your personal preference. But things can change from wave to wave at some surf locations.

If someone is dropping in, you may decide at the last minute to go in the opposite direction – but only if the wave is wedge shaped and is forming nicely in both directions.

3. The Take-Off Position

When a wave is approaching, turn and start to paddle for the wave when it is about a metre and half away (6 feet) from you and as the wave forms up to a peak. <u>Feel the momentum of the wave take you</u>. (You are now at the "take-off" point).

Prior to take-off, you should be positioned in the best possible place. This is where the waves start to form up before breaking. You will also usually be competing with other surfers to catch the waves. Remember not to "drop in" on other surfers. (refer to *Learn to Surf for Beginners* manual for more on "dropping in").

If the wave is breaking both left and right, call out "left" or "right" to let others know which direction you intend to surf the wave.

You should also watch out for other surfers paddling out and jockeying for position. They can get in your way. If this happens, you might need to whistle or shout out to others or abort the take-off.

The best way to abort the take-off is to use the 3 P's method:
- **<u>pushing</u> and leaning back** towards the tail of your board
- **<u>put your legs</u>** in the water off either side of the board (provides anchor/drag)
- **<u>place your arms and hands</u>** in water, and start back paddling

Surf Study - Aborting
the Take-off

The sequence of photo's below show a surfer taking-off. The surfer then notices other surfers have moved across into his line of surfing.

1 Surfer at the take-off point. When paddling for this wave, the way was probably clear for the surfer.

2 Now the surfer sees that other surfers are blocking his path. He attempts to abort the take-off by pushing back i.e. sit up, place hands to rails, and <u>pushes</u> and leans back on the back of surfboard, so the wave can pass him by.

3 The surfer is sitting up more, has <u>put his legs in the water</u> (as in the sitting position) and is pulling back off the wave by moving all body weight to the tail of the board.

4 Surfer now <u>puts arms and hands</u> in water to back paddle. He has successfully pulled out of the take-off. The wave moves ahead without him and a potentially dangerous collision has been averted.

3.1 Choose a Landmark

Your ability to choose the right place to take-off will greatly assist in whether you catch the waves or not.

Most surfers will, at sometime, use landmarks to help identify the best take-off point in the line up.

You need to choose two landmark points that you can line up so that when you are in the water, you are certain you are in the correct place. If you only choose one landmark, you will be able to see the landmark from a number of places however you will not know if you are in the exact position every time.

As you paddle out, always be checking where the waves are breaking. Then, as you continue to paddle out, look back towards the shore and see where you are on the shoreline. Try to pick two landmark points that line up. The landmarks can be anything - palm trees, hills, buildings, stalls or anything that is fixed, that you can see from the water.

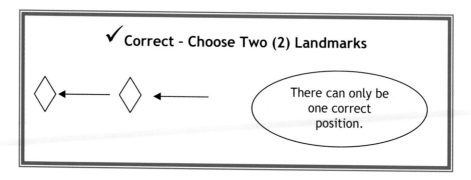

✓ **Correct - Choose Two (2) Landmarks**

There can only be one correct position.

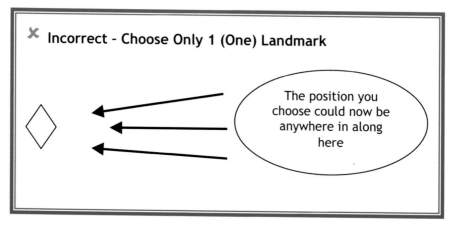

✗ **Incorrect - Choose Only 1 (One) Landmark**

The position you choose could now be anywhere in along here

When you are in the water, the waves can look quite different as to where they could be breaking. Landmarks are an extra aid – especially in larger surf.

The landmarks will also help you know if you are drifting too far from the take-off position.

You may not always be able to choose landmarks at all breaks. If the swells are coming in from different angles, the take-off point can be at different places for each wave.

Sometimes you may choose two sets of landmarks especially when the sets are coming through in two distinctive sizes – e.g. larger swells (out further and right) and small swell sets (in closer and to the left).

3.2 Feathering

Feathering is when the crest of the wave starts to fray and turn white. It occurs on waves as they start to stand up, before throwing over. Looking for signs of feathering also helps assist the surfer identify the best take-off point on the wave. Paddle over to the place where the wave is feathering so that you can turn and catch the waves at that point.

Feathering only occurs when the wind is off-shore. Feathering does not occur when the wind is on-shore. An on-shore wind will cause waves to crumble.

4. Catching the Wave

Once you <u>feel the momentum of the wave take you</u>, you can stand up on the board. ***Not before***.

The speed at which you get to your feet will become more important. For example, if you take a very fast hollow wave, the speed you jump to your feet will determine whether you make the take-off or not. If you are too slow to your feet, the wave will throw you over - more than likely pitching you over the falls.

4.1 Taking the Drop

When you catch a wave, you will take "the drop". This is the initial drop from the crest of the wave to the trough of the wave.

The drop is where you gain the speed necessary to do your first turn. The higher the drop, the more speed you will gain.

The size of the drop depends on swell size and any rips or currents running in the surf at the time.

Your ability to handle the drop on all types of waves will greatly assist your chances in catching the waves and riding them well.

5. Riding the Wave

Riding the waves will require balance, correct position and stance and lots of practice. Let's have a look at some of these in more detail.

5.1 Positioning on the Wave

There are terms to describe sections of the wave and therefore where you would be riding on the wave.

Inside Section
Is the last part of the wave closest to the beach/shore. Also called a shore-break.

Middle Section
The middle part of a longer wave – not the beginning or end.

Outside Section
Where the wave is initially breaking.

5.2 Fore-hand and Back-hand

Fore-hand and back-hand are terms to describe the way you stand towards the wave. If you are riding a wave, you will either be riding fore-hand or back-hand, depending on whether you take a left-hand wave or a right-hand wave.

5.2.1 Fore-hand

This means you will be riding with your body facing into the wave (as pictured here).

5.2.2 Back-hand

This means you will be riding with your back facing the wave (as pictured here).

If you are a natural foot surfer (left foot in front of right), you ride on your fore-hand on a right-hand wave (photo 5.2.1 above). You will be riding on your back-hand on a left-hand wave (photo 5.2.2 above).

If you are a goofy foot surfer (right foot in front of left), the opposite of the above applies.

Some people are "switch foot" surfers. This means they can ride either goofy or natural foot and are able to switch to their fore-hand on any wave they ride. They are still usually more competent and comfortable in their natural stance.

It is generally easier to ride on your fore-hand. This is because:
• when turning you are learning forward over your feet. Turning on your back-hand requires you to lean backwards over your heels (this is difficult for some people).
• it is easier to tuck up into the curl of the wave for tube rides.

Whether you like to ride back-hand or fore-hand comes down to personal preference. Some surfers prefer to ride on their back-hand as they feel more comfortable that way. By trial and error, you will find out what works best for you.

5.3 Stance

At the intermediate level, maintaining the correct stance on your surfboard is one of the major factors in you being able to progress and surf well. Always remember to maintain the correct stance when standing. We covered this in detail in the *Learn to Surfer for Beginners* manual. Remember:

1. **Your knees should remain bent** <u>at all times</u>. This allows your knees and legs to act as shock absorbers in all types of waves and conditions that you are likely to encounter.

2. **Your feet should be apart, roughly shoulder width or slightly wider.** This allows you to maintain a good centre of balance and be ready to turn the board and perform manoeuvres.

3. **Your arms should be outstretched, from your sides**, slightly bent at the elbows, not rigid. This will help you to balance and assist in turning.

4. **Your eyes should be focusing on the section of wave just in front of you.** This allows you to assess how the wave is forming up and then to take action accordingly.

✓ **Correct Stance**

These surfers look totally in control of the surfboard. No matter how the wave forms up, the surfer is ready.

✖ Incorrect Stance

Note the poor stance of this surfer. This surfer's legs are almost extended and he doesn't have his centre of gravity down over and through his feet. (His knees should be bent and he should be leaning slightly forward).

This surfer eventually falls backwards off the surfboard.

5.4 Using Your Body Weight

Using your body weight, when surfing, is critical to surfing effectively. The movement and pressure of different parts of your body (especially your arms) allows you to turn the board. It is also important when performing manoeuvres. We talk more about using your body weight in the *Learn to Surf - Advanced level* manual.

5.5 Speed

The speed at which your surfboard moves allows you to keep up with the peeling lip and to perform manoeuvres at different places on the wave.

The drop in the wave will help you gain initial speed. The steeper the drop, the more speed you can gain. Different turns and manoeuvres, performed at the correct timing and location on a wave, will also help to maintain or even produce more speed.

You often see people bouncing (hopping) on their board on the wave to keep up their speed and stay with the wave. More skilled surfers do not need to bounce on their board as much. They look for drops where the wave is forming up in front of them and then turn to take advantage of the drop to gain their speed.

5.6 Turning your Board

At the beginner's level, you learned to turn the surfboard by leaning your body weight in the direction you wanted to turn. You would have been able to gradually turn up and down along the wave face. At the intermediate level, your ability to turn your surfboard and the degree of your turn will affect your ability to perform manoeuvres.

To turn your surfboard effectively, you should be on a wave at some speed. Turning will involve a combination of feet and lower body movement and upper body movement, all performed simultaneously.

5.6.1 Feet and Lower Body Movement

1. At speed, lift your front foot slightly (keep contact with the board) to release pressure and allow the front of the board to lift slightly.
2. This will put slightly more pressure over your back foot.
3. Lean over in the direction you want the board to turn.
4. If you are on your fore-hand, exert pressure down through your knees and over your toes. On your back-hand, exert pressure down through your knees and over your heels.
5. Use the back foot to pivot the board around into the turn. (The more pressure over your back foot, the sharper the turn.)
6. Use the front foot to control the direction and degree of the turn.

5.6.2 Upper Body Movement

The upper body is also moving at the same time as you are applying feet and lower body movements. When you are about to turn, at speed on the wave:
* Turn your head in the direction you want to turn.
* Remember to lean over at an angle that will keep your body's G forces pushing down through the centre of your board.
* Swing your arms around in the direction of the turn. The more pronounced the swinging of your arms the sharper the turn will be.
* This brings your hips and waist around in the direction of the turn.
* Your legs and surfboard will follow.

You will be turning your surfboard either on your fore-hand or your back-hand. The principles are similar. On your fore-hand, you will be leaning forward, over your toes, into the turn. On your back-hand, you will be leaning back into your heels. Let's see this in sequence.

Surf Study - Turning the Surfboard on your Fore-hand

1   Turn your head in the direction you want to turn. Just before reaching the place where you want to begin to turn, put slightly more pressure over your back foot.

2   Use your front foot to guide the board into the turn. Keep your knees bent and ready to push off.

3   Begin to lean over into your turn allowing the front of the board to lift slightly. Continue to lean over in the direction you want the board to turn. Use the back foot to guide the board off the tail, into the turn.

4   Continue to lean over and drive your turn whilst swinging your arms around in the direction of the turn. Your arms help to maintain your body's balance and bring your hips and waist in the direction of the turn. Your legs and surfboard will follow. Continue to exert force down through your legs and feet into the board and out into your turn.

5   Use pressure over your front foot to control the sharpness of the turn. The amount of pressure over your front foot and the angle of that pressure will determine the degree of the turn.

Surf Study - Turning
the Surfboard on your Back-hand

1   Turn your head in the direction you want to turn. Just before reaching the place where you want to begin to turn, put slightly more pressure over your back foot.

2   Use your front foot to guide the board into the turn. Keep your knees bent and ready to push off.

3   Begin to lean over into your turn allowing the front of the board to lift slightly. Continue to lean over in the direction you want the board to turn. Use the back foot to guide the board off the tail, into the turn.

4   Continue to lean over and drive your turn whilst swinging your arms around in the direction of the turn. Your arms help to maintain your body's balance and bring your hips and waist in the direction of the turn. Your legs and surfboard will follow. Continue to exert force down through your legs and feet into the board and out into your turn.

5   Use pressure over your front foot to control the sharpness of the turn. The amount of pressure over your front foot and the angle of that pressure will determine the degree of the turn.

6. Getting Off the Wave

6.1 Bailing

If you see a wave closing out in front of you, you can dive, or jump, off the board. This is referred to as "bailing", as in "bail out".

If you have to bail, try to dive/jump off underneath the lip. This way you will be out of the full force and impact zone of the wave. You pop up out behind the wave with your board dragging through the wave behind you. Be careful of leg-rope recoil. Come up with your hands first. Before bailing, look out for other surfers/swimmers, to make sure your surfboard does not hit them.

At a reef break, be aware of how shallow the water is. If you bail at a reef break, dive anywhere but underneath the force of the lip (impact zone). Otherwise, you may be driven into the bottom of the reef by the lip and end up with some injuries.

<u>Do not dive too deeply</u>. In some cases, if the water is very shallow, you may also need to dive very shallow. i.e. dive just under the water's surface. Don't go too deep. Then swim out toward the back of the wave toward the deeper water.

<u>Remember not to kick off the bottom </u>when surfing over reef breaks. Reefs can be very sharp and you could easily cut your feet. Booties help protect your feet. It is also a good idea for the <u>intermediate surfer</u> to wear a protective helmet in big waves over rock/reef breaks.

6.2 Turn Off

This is where you turn up and off the face of the wave.

You can turn off a wave at any time. However, you would more than likely turn up off the wave just before it closes out on you. To turn off a wave, lean your body in the direction you want to turn thereby directing you and your board up and off the back of the wave.

6.3 Flick Off

Before leg-ropes had been invented, surfers used, and perfected, a technique called the "flick off". This was used when a surfer wanted to get off a wave, without having to swim to shore to retrieve their surfboard. The surfer would flick their surfboard up off the wave into the open water behind the wave.

This usually meant the board would float on the water behind the wave and not be washed into the shore. The surfer only had to swim a short distance to retrieve their board.

The flick off is still used to get off a wave that is closing out. You can flick your board up and over at the same time as you dive through the face or under the wave.

Be careful not to hit other surfers around you.

7. Wiping Out

At the intermediate level, you will come across numerous ways to wipe out!

The worst type of wipe-out (in bigger waves) is where you get "lip launched". The lip catches you and the board and throws you over the falls. More than likely you will come down in the impact zone where you can be held under water and tumbled around quite a bit. Your surfboard can also be broken if the full force of the wave hits your board.

To avoid wipe-outs, avoid getting caught by the lip as it peels over. You can do this by turning down in front of the wave or try to turn off the back of the wave before it closes out on you. As you turn up and under the lip, try to grab the front rail of your board to help pull your board through the back of the wave.

Sometimes you may decide you need to bail if you feel that you are going to wipe-out. Once again, remember to dive off the board correctly, as described above. i.e. under the lip and out to the back of the wave.

Always be aware of other surfers/swimmers close by as your board may fly out and hit them.

When you wipe-out:

- Remain calm
- Don't fight against the tumbling wave – just go with it. The wave's energy will pass by you.
- You can curl up into a ball on larger waves.
- Don't resist being pulled through the water by your leg-rope.
- Try to swim to the surface of the water, or find your leg-rope and pull on this to help bring yourself to the surface.
- Come back to the surface hand first if you feel tension through your leg-rope.

Learning to ride the wave properly and manoeuvring yourself into the correct position, will help minimise any wipe-outs.

CHAPTER 10
Surfing Manoeuvres

Outcomes

☐ Display appropriate balance and confidence when demonstrating methods of manoeuvring and intermediate surfing manoeuvres on small, spilling unbroken waves:
- Top turn
- Bottom turn
- Cut-back
- Re-entry

☐ Demonstrate traversing along the green face of a spilling wave.
☐ Demonstrate turning and linking of basic manoeuvres.

Performing surf manoeuvres is all part of the fun and thrill of surfing. There is nothing more exciting than when you complete a perfect manoeuvre.

Surfing manoeuvres are performed not only for the fun of it, but can be essential to help you keep up with the speed of the breaking wave.

In order to surf on a wave, you must have enough drive off the wave to push you along. This usually means staying close to the curl of the wave. The curl is the place where the most energy is generated. However, you may often be in positions where you are not near the curl of the wave. It is then necessary to build speed which will drive you back to the curl.

You will often see surfers turning back (cutting back) on waves. The reason for this is to stay as close to the curl as possible. There are a few different manoeuvres that can be performed to get a surfer back to the wave curl.

Manoeuvres are generally performed in a particular sequence.

For example, it is generally difficult to take off at the top of a wave and do a quick re-entry straight away. Usually, you must first go down the wave, to get some speed, do a bottom turn to generate speed to go back up to the top of the wave. You can then hit the lip, perform a re-entry and then continue along the wave perhaps driving out in front of the curl far enough and with enough speed to go into a nice cut-back. This will then drive you back towards the breaking curl of the wave where you will regain the wave's power to drive you down again and into your next manoeuvre.

The standard manoeuvres at the intermediate level are:
- bottom turn
- top turn
- cut-back
- re-entry

Once you have learned these manoeuvres, you can then start to perform them at greater speed, with more power, and learn to position yourself in a more critical place on a wave so that you can continue on the wave rather than stop dead in the flat water.

You can then start to learn the more advanced manoeuvres such as roundhouse cutbacks, snaps and tube rides. These manoeuvres require a more in-depth knowledge of the mechanics of surfing which are all covered in the *Learn to Surf - Advanced Level* manual.

1. Trimming

Trimming is one of the most basic manoeuvres. We discussed this in the *Learn to Surf for Beginners* manual. It is where you are positioned at, or near, the shoulder of the breaking wave. You ride across the wave, not turning at all (can also be called "holding a line").

Being able to trim effectively is important. It can help you to catch up and keep pace with the breaking wave rather than getting left behind in the foam. It also allows you to build speed to get past sections of the wave or to set yourself up for your next manoeuvre.

2. Bottom Turn

The bottom turn is performed at the trough or "bottom" of the wave. Hence, it is called the "bottom turn". It is usually the first turn you perform after you have taken off on a wave.

Once you have taken a wave, you ideally want to build up as much speed as possible. So you head down to the trough of the wave. The bigger the drop down the wave, the more speed you will gain.

Once you reach the bottom of the wave, the wave will probably pass you by, or knock you off, if you do not turn to get back onto the face of the wave.

As you near the bottom of the wave, you should start your turn. Ideally, you will have built up enough speed to propel you through the turn and back up onto the wave face.

The speed at which you can go into the turn and the amount you lean into your turn will depend on your level of ability.

When you are first learning this turn, you will begin by performing smaller bottom turns where you have only built up a minimal amount of speed. You may not be taking off down the wave too steeply but more likely on an angled take-off across the wave face.

Things that can go wrong when performing a bottom turn are:

- leaning too hard and falling off into the wave face.
- leaning over without having enough speed. This will cause you to fall off.
- grabbing a rail in the water (i.e. the water is holding the rail) resulting in you not being able to turn the board. This generally happens when you do not have enough speed or you put too much weight over your front foot.
- going too far out in front of the wave before turning (losing speed). When you turn, you will come to a stop. The wave will catch up to you and knock you off your board.

Surf Study - Performing
a Bottom Turn

1   Take off and head down the wave to the bottom/trough of the wave. Be sure you are in a crouching position (knees bent) as you are dropping down the wave.

2   As you reach the bottom of the wave, you should be crouched at maximum position. Start to lean over into your turn (ready to spring).

3   Continue to lean over into the turn. Once you are half way through your turn, flex your legs to straighten (like a spring uncoiling), pushing hard off the base of the wave and driving yourself up onto the wave face again.

4   Use the pressure over your front foot to control the sharpness of the turn. As you head for your next manoeuvre, your body recoils again (knees bent) ready to push off the next turn.

3. Top Turn

A top turn is performed near the top of the wave. There is less force being exerted than that being exerted at a bottom turn usually making the top turn easier to perform.

A top turn is generally performed:

- as you reach the top of the wave.
- when you don't have time to go straight to the bottom of the wave. This occurs when a wave is breaking quickly and you need to keep up with a fast peeling lip.
- to avoid another surfer paddling out in the line up.

Things that can go wrong when performing a top turn are:

- you could grab an edge of your leading rail when leaning too much into the turn, without enough speed – causing you to fall off.

Surf Study - Performing
a Top Turn

1 Head up towards the top of the wave. Just before reaching the top of the wave, transfer slightly more pressure over your back foot.

2 Use your front foot to guide the board into the turn. Allow the front of the board to lift slightly, swinging your arms into your turn. The back foot is used to pivot the board around into the turn. The front foot controls the sharpness of the turn.

3 Lean your body over into the turn down the wave face.

4 The board will naturally turn in the direction you are leaning and pushing.

4. Cut-Back

A cut-back is the same as a top turn however the turn is continued bringing you around and back towards the curling wave.

You would perform a cut-back in order to regain the momentum necessary to continue on the wave. When you are surfing, you may generate so much speed that you find yourself placed well in front of the breaking wave. At this point, the water is flatter (wave has faded, out into deeper water, or not yet formed up) and has less energy resulting in you losing speed/energy.

To regain momentum, you should return to the steeper part of the wave near the breaking curl. If the wave continues to form up in front of you, this eliminates the need for a cutback as you have continual fall and face on the wave to generate speed and momentum.

Things that can go wrong when performing a cut-back are:

- leaning too hard and far over into your turn without enough speed, resulting in you falling off.

- go too far out in front of the wave and end up in flat water. At this point, you run out of speed to get back to the energy source of the wave (the curl).

- When leaning over into the turn, the rail can catch in the water and track (like a railway line). Therefore stopping you from performing the arc of your turn and resulting in you wiping out.

Surf Study - Performing
a Cut-back

1   At speed out in front of the breaking curl, when you then decide to cut-back.

2   Begin to shift your weight over your back foot and lighten the pressure down through your front foot (guiding foot). Start to lean into the cut-back.

3   Twist your upper body and arms around into the turn. Continue leaning into the cut-back as you bring the surfboard around.

4   Use light pressure on your front foot to control the extent of the cut-back. (i.e. how far you take the turn).

5. Re-Entry

A re-entry is a top turn performed at speed where the front part of the board goes up above the lip of the wave.

A re-entry is performed to stay at the source of the energy of the wave. The closer the surfer stays at the curl of the wave, the more speed and energy the surfer will continue to have.

The manoeuvre also allows the surfer to turn faster as the surfer is turning the board off the tail only (as the front of the board is above the lip). It also means there is no chance of the front rail grabbing thereby assisting you to stay on your surfboard.

The re-entry is a more spectacular manoeuvre than a top turn - resulting in the surfer hitting the lip of the wave and sending off a big spray!

Things that can go wrong when performing a re-entry are:

- As you head up the face of the wave to hit the lip, you can leave your re-entry (turn) too late. This can result in the fins coming out of the water (loosing your fins), losing all control and landing on your face in the wave.

- As you swing the front of your board around, you can sometimes catch the front leading edge of the rail in the lip of the wave, throwing you off your board.

- If you perform the re-entry too slowly, then the curling wave and open wave face will go past you.

1 Head up the wave aiming for the lip. Begin to shift your weight to the back foot.

2 As you are about to hit the lip, lean over hard into your turn (apply full pressure on your back foot and guide with the front foot). Twist the top of your body to face back down the wave.

3 Pivot the back of your board at 180 degrees. You will be turning on the spot - off the tail.

4 A big spray of water may go into the air from the lip - depending on the speed (power) of your turn.

5 Drop back down the face and continue on the wave.

6. Linking Manoeuvres

Your ability to link manoeuvres, based on the particular wave conditions, will determine your ability to ride the waves.

Let's have a look at some surfers riding waves.

Surf Study 1 - Surfing The Wave

1 The surfer drops down the wave and leans into a bottom turn.

2 This drives him back up onto the wave face.

3 He then straightens out to get further down, along the wave.

4 He now leans into a cut-back to stay right at the curl (power of the wave).

5 He, again, drops down the wave face.

6 Pushes off into another bottom turn.

7 The surfer is now up and on the face of the wave and heads to the top of the wave.

8 He leans back into another cutback to stay at the curl (power source of the wave).

9 The surfer, again, drops back down the face of the wave.

10 He readies himself to push off on another bottom turn.

11 The wave gets smaller and surfer decides to exit the wave.

Surf Study 2 - Surfing
The Wave

1 The surfer takes off down through the whitewash.

2 Surfer drops down to the bottom of the wave.

3 Surfer leans over into her bottom turn (guiding with the front foot).

4 Surfer rides across, up onto the wave face.

5 Surfer does a slight top turn and is crouched ready for her next manoeuvre.

6 Surfer drops down to the bottom of the wave again and runs through a little section.

7 Surfer leans over and pushes into a bottom turn.

8 Surfer rides back up onto the face of the wave.

9 Surfer leans back into a cut-back.

10 Surfer continues into her cut-back.

11 The curling lip and white water have caught up which helps push the surfer down out in front of the wave again.

12 Surfer leans over again into a slight bottom turn and turns up across the wave as it fades out.

Surf Study 3 - Surfing
The Wave

1 After doing a bottom turn and racing out on the open face, surfer begins to lean into a cut-back.

2 Surfer continues to lean over into the cut-back. Weight is over the back foot and front foot is guiding the board.

3 Surfer drives back towards the curling wave.

4 Before hitting the curl of the white water, surfer begins to lean back again towards the open face of the wave.

5 Surfer continues leaning back towards the open face as the curl of the wave catches up to him and begins to push him.

6 Surfer drops down onto the face of the wave through the white water.

7 As surfer hits the clean water at the bottom of the wave, he leans back into his bottom turn. (Notice the crouched stance ready to push off the feet again.)

8 Surfer drives back up along the face underneath the lip (which is now peeling over).

9 As the surfer comes up underneath the lip of the curling wave, he crouches down and holds the outside rail of the board with his back hand. As the surfer is moving very fast, and high up in the curl, this stance will help him to maintain his high line along the wave and to tuck up under the curling lip (tube-riding).

10 As the lip closes down on the surfer (no tube), the fact that he has held the rail of the board will help him to maintain his balance rather than being pushed off the board and being wiped out.

11 The surfer is now under the broken wave (a cover-up) but still driving forwards along the wave.

12 The surfer emerges from under the broken foam and leans forward over his front foot ready to drop back down the wave.

13 He sees the wave the wave has entered into deeper water and fades out.

Conclusion

If you follow the basic steps through this instruction manual you should be able to start to catch waves with a reasonable amount of confidence.

You will be able to progress on to a higher level with continued practice on any areas you feel you are not fully proficient at as yet.

Keep surfing and enjoy the ocean with everyone.

Share the waves.

Surfing Terms

Ankle strap	Part of the leg-rope (leash). The part that wraps around your ankle.
Back-hand	Term used to describe riding on the wave with your back facing into the wave.
Backwash	Wave washes up on the shore or into the land and then forms back into a wave again as it washes out to sea.
Bailing	Diving off the surfboard.
Bank	Sand underneath where the waves break. Also referred to as sandbank.
Beach break	Surf breaking, over sandbanks, and into a beach
Booties	Rubber foot cover worn by surfers to protect feet from the cold and/or damage caused from reef/rocks.
Bombora	Surf that breaks out at sea (away from the coastline) - over submerged rock or reef formation. Also referred to as "bombie".
Bottom	Underneath part of the surfboard.
Bottom turn	Turn performed at the bottom of the wave.
Centre deck pad	Thin pad on centre of surfboard to provide grip when standing on the board. Used as a wax alternative.
Channel	Deep section of water formed by a rip or current. Sometimes called "gully".
Channels	Ridged design found on bottom of some surfboards.
Close out	Wave that stands up and throws over, all at one time, with a great force. Also referred to as a "plunging wave" or "dumper".
Concave	Spoon-like design found on bottom of some surfboards.
Cross-shore wind	Wind that blows sideways across incoming surf.
Crowded	Many people in the water making it difficult to catch waves.
Current	A body of water that usually moves out to sea or across the shore. Also referred to as a "rip".
Cutback	Surfing manoeuvre. A turn that takes the surfer back toward the breaking part of the wave curl.
Deck	Top of the surfboard where you stand.
Deck pad	Pad on surfboard to provide grip when standing on the board. Also referred to as grip.
Ding	Damage to the surfboard.
Double up	Occurs when one wave travelling to the shore, catches up to another wave creating one larger size wave.
Drop	Refers to the fall in wave face.
Dropping in	Surfing etiquette rule that relates to who has the right to ride on the wave. The surfer who is up and riding closest to the curl (on the

inside) is entitled to the wave.

Duck dive	Manoeuvre to negotiate through a wave. The surfer pushes self and board under the broken wave.
Dumper	Wave that stands up and throws over, all at one time, with a great force. Also referred to as a "plunging wave" or "close out".
Eskimo roll	Manoeuvre to negotiate through a wave. The surfer rolls self and board through the broken wave. Also called a "roll over".
Fade	Wave face is diminishing into deeper water.
Feathering	Where the crest of the wave starts to fray and turn white.
Fins	Guiding rudders of the surfboard.
Fin box	Place on surfboard where removable fins are locked into place.
Fin system	Removable fins allowing you to change shapes, size, transport, etc.
Fish tail	Type of surfboard tail design.
Flick off	When riding on the wave, manoeuvre to get off the wave. Where you flick your surfboard up off the wave into open water behind the wave.
Flex	The amount of movement in the fin, under sideways pressure, when riding the board.
Foam	The broken part of the wave. Also referred to as "whitewash".
Fore-hand	Term used to describe riding on the wave with your body facing into the wave.
Foil	The tapering of the thickness of the board, from nose to tail.
Forms up	When a wave starts to build up.
Full suit	Wetsuit that has long arms and long legs. Can also get a short arm full suit. Also known as a "steamer".
Fun board	Surfboard same shape as a Malibu with a length under 8 foot. Also known as a "mini mal.
Glassy	Smooth water that glistens from the reflection of the light.
Gloves	Rubber hand cover worn by the surfer to protect from the cold and/or to assist in paddling.
Goofy foot	Standing on the surfboard with the right foot forward.
Grip	Thin pad on surfboard to provide traction when standing on board.
Grommet	Very young surfer.
Ground swell	Swell generated by wind from strong deep low pressure system/s out at sea.
Gun	Short board shape, more tapered towards the nose and tail. Length above 7 - 9 foot or more.
Holding a line	Riding across the wave, straight towards a point ahead of you on the wave.
Hollow	Wave that has a space between the wave face and the water that is throwing over. Tube rides are possible with this type of wave.

Hood	Head cover, made from wetsuit material, used to keep your head warm.
Inside	Closest to the breaking curl.
Inside section	Last part of the wave closest to the shore. Also called a "shore break".
Impact zone	Where all the force of the wave will come down as it throws over.
Length	The length of the surfboard, along the stringer, from nose to tail.
Leash	Specially designed cord that connects you and the surfboard. The leash is attached to your ankle at one end and at the board, into the plug, at the other end. Also called a leg-rope.
Leash cord	Part of leg-rope (leash). Connects to the rail saver at one end and the ankle strap at the other end.
Left hand wave	Wave breaks to the right, as you look from the shore.
Leg-rope	Specially designed cord that connects you and the surfboard. The leg-rope is attached to your ankle at one end and at the board, into the plug, at the other end. Also called a leash.
Lip	The top or crest of the wave. The thin part of a wave that rises up then throws out and over.
Lip launched	A wipe-out where the lip of the wave catches you and the board and throws you over the falls.
Long board	A long, wide surfboard with rounded nose. Length usually around 8 foot and over. Also known as a "Malibu".
Loose	Term to describe manoeuvrability of some surfboards. The more loose the board, the more manoeuvrable.
Lull	A period of no waves occurring in between sets.
Lumpy	Bumps and ripples moving on the wave's surface.
Malibu	A long, wide surfboard with rounded nose. Length usually around 8 foot and over. Also known as a "long board".
Messy	Wave with little form as a result of wind blowing either across or on-shore. Also known as "mushie".
Middle section	The middle part of a longer wave - not the beginner or end.
Mini mal	Surfboard same shape as a Malibu with a length under 9 foot. Also known as a "fun board".
Mushie	Wave with little form as a result of wind blowing either across or on-shore. Also known as "messy".
Natural foot	Standing on the surfboard with your left foot forward.
Nose	Front section of the surfboard.
Nose dive	This is where the nose (front) of a surfboard digs into the water's surface and causes the board to stall. Also referred to as "pearling".
Nose pad	Thin rubber pad on nose of surfboard to provide traction when standing on the board.
Off-shore wind	Wind that blows from the land to the ocean.

On-shore wind	Wind that blows from the ocean to the land.
Outline	Overall area of the surfboard, as viewed from above. Also referred to as "shape", "plan shape".
Outside	Wave breaking further out to sea.
Outside section	Where the wave is initially breaking.
Over the falls	This will happen when you catch a wave and catch it too late, the wave throws you over resulting in a wipe out. Also referred to as "getting pitched".
Peaking	A wave forms up into a wedge shape before breaking.
Pearling	This is where the nose (front) of a surfboard digs into the water's surface and causes the board to stall. Also referred to as "nose dive".
Peeling off / over	The wave breaks perfectly. i.e. wave will stand up cleanly, not diminishing and gently peeling over from left to right or right to left.
Pin tail	Type of surfboard tail design - tapered pointy shape.
Plan shape	Overall area of the surfboard, as viewed from above. Also referred to as "shape", "outline".
Plunging wave	Wave that stands up and the top throws over with a great force. Also referred to as a "dumper". Not suitable for surfing.
Plug	Where leg-rope is attached to the surfboard.
Point break	Surf that breaks down along a headland.
Rail saver	Part of the leg-rope (leash). Protects the rails from damage.
Rails	The edge (side) of the surfboard between deck and bottom.
Rash vest	T-shirt type of material to help prevent rash and protect from the sun.
Reef break	Surf that breaks over a submerged reef or rocky formation.
Re-entry	Surfing manoeuvre. A top turn performed at speed where the front part of the board goes up above the lip of the wave.
Reform	Breaking wave that fades as it goes over deeper water and then forms into a wave again as it moves over shallower water.
Right hand wave	Wave breaks to the left, as you look from the shore.
Rip	A body of water that usually moves out to sea or across the shore. Also referred to as a "current".
Rocker	The curve in the board (from nose to tail) when looking from the side angle.
Roll-over	Manoeuvre to negotiate through a wave. Often referred to as an Eskimo roll.
Rounded pin tail	Type of surfboard tail design.
Rounded square tail	Type of surfboard tail design.
Round tail	Type of surfboard tail design.

Sandbank	Sand underneath shallow water where the waves break.
Section	Part of the wave.
Set	A group of waves.
Shape	Overall area of the surfboard. Also referred to as "outline" and plan shape.
Shore break	The last part of the wave closest to the shore. Also called the "inside section."
Short john	Wetsuit that has short legs and no arms.
Short board	Light-weight, thinner surfboard, not as wide as Malibu, more pointed nose, length under 7 foot.
Single fin	One fin surfboard.
Snake	When a surfer paddles to the inside of a break when others have already been waiting to catch the waves there.
Spilling wave	When the top of the wave gently topples down the front of the wave. Suitable for surfing.
Spring suit	Wetsuit that has short legs and short arms.
Soft cover	Cover for surfboard. Used mostly for local travel. Made from thin material.
Soup	The broken part (white water) of the wave.
Spitting	Fine spray of water forced out the end of a tubing wave.
String cord	Part of the leg-rope (leash). Attaches the leg-rope (leash) to the plug in the surfboard.
Stringer	The timber strip that runs down the centre of the surfboard providing strength.
Steamer	Wetsuit with long arms and long legs. Also known as a "full suit". Can also get a short arm steamer.
Step	A wave forms within a wave creating a ledge in the wave face.
Sucky	Wave that occurs alongside a fast moving rip/current. Wave has a much faster continuous drop down the wave face.
Surf cap	Cap to wear when surfing to keep the sun off your face and protect you from sunburn.
Surf Helmet	Helmet made from light plastic. Worn by the surfer to protect head.
Swallow tail	Type of surfboard tail design.
Sweet spot	The area, when standing on your surfboard, where it will perform.
Swell	The formation of waves.
Switch foot	Surfer who has the ability to change their leading foot. Can ride natural or goofy foot.
Swivel	Part of the leg-rope (leash). Usually two swivels - one at each end of the leash cord and helps prevent tangling.
Tail	Back section of the surfboard.
Tail pad	Thin rubber pad on tail of surfboard to provide traction when standing

on the board.

Take-off point	The place where you take off on the wave.
Thickness	The thickness of the surfboard, usually measured from the centre or the thickest part of the board.
Throwing over	The wave as it breaks over.
Thruster	Three fin surfboard.
Tide watch	A watch that shows the rising and falling tide times.
Tight	Term to describe manoeuvrability of some surfboards. The more tight the board, the less manoeuvrable.
Tide chart	A chart that shows high and low tides with dates and times.
Top turn	Turn performed near the top of the wave.
Travel cover	A protective cover for surfboard. Used for travelling long distances.
Trimming	Riding across the wave, straight toward a point ahead of you on the wave. Also referred to as "holding a line".
Trough	The base/bottom of the wave.
Turn off	Where you turn up off the face of the wave.
Twin fin	Two fin surfboard.
Uneven	"Lumpy" waves.
Vee	Wedge shape design found on the bottom of some surfboards.
Walling up	The wave as it builds/forms up before breaking.
Wave curl	The lip of the wave as it peels over (the breaking part of the wave).
Wave face	The concave unbroken part of a wave where most manoeuvres can be performed.
Wax	Special surfboard wax put on surfboard to provide traction when standing on the board.
Wax comb	Special comb used to scratch up your wax cover on your surfboard.
Webbed gloves	Gloves with web between fingers. (Assists in paddling).
Wetsuit	Flexible rubber clothing that hugs the body to keep you warm in cool/cold water.
Wind blown	Wave with little form as a result of wind blowing either across or on-shore.
Wind swell	Swell generate by wind.
Wipe out	Falling off when riding a wave.
Whitewash	The broken part (white water) of the wave. Also referred to as "foam".